D1254430

Structured Java
An Introductory Course in Java

Structured Java
An Introductory Course in Java

Glen K. Blood

Published 2017

Copyright © 2017 by Glen K. Blood

All rights reserved. No part of this publication may be reproduced, distributed, or transmitted in any form or by any means, including photocopying, recording, or other electronic or mechanical methods, without the prior written permission of the publisher, except in the case of brief quotations embodied in critical reviews and certain other noncommercial uses permitted by copyright law. For permission requests, write to the publisher, addressed "Attention: Permissions Coordinator," at the address below.

Glen K. Blood
260 Villager Drive
Saint Simons Island, GA 31522

gblood@ccga.edu

Second Edition 2017

ISBN 978-1-365-86676-0

Table of Contents

ix

Introduction

Welcome. This book was developed after a few semesters teaching the Computer Science programming courses at the Coastal College of Georgia. Using Java as an introductory language has been a challenge. I have come to the realization that starting with classes and objects leads to confusion with my students when they haven't mastered the basic logic structures and method calls of the language.

Computers are stupid. They understand two things, zero and one. However, they understand these two things, extremely fast. It was up to mathematicians, engineers, and programmers to teach computers how to do things.

Over the years, many computer languages have been developed. Either for a specific purpose, such as controlling a plane, or to make software development easier (the infamous Silver Bullet). One of those languages is Java. I will not get into a History lesson, or political or religious discussion. In case you are new to the field, many of our product discussions take on a religious fervor. If you do not believe me, try getting into an Apple versus Microsoft debate.

Most modern languages can be placed in one of two camps. Procedural (aka Functional) or Object Oriented Languages. There are others, such as Lisp (Recursive), SQL (Set-based), etc., but they are for another day.

Procedural languages are based on breaking your problem into small tight understandable processes (called Modules, Methods, Procedures, or Functions depending on the Language) and using those processes to solve your problem. The paradigm is based on the process. These can best be seen by the Structure Chart:

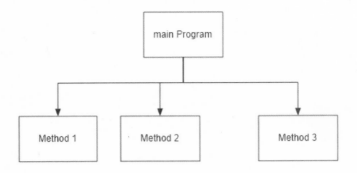

Java is an Object-Oriented Language. This means that it is based on the idea that everything in software can be started with a Template called a **Class** which has attributes (aka **variables**) and can take actions (aka **methods**). Most of these classes must be brought to life or instantiated as **Objects** before they can be used. A Class can be a Car, which has attributes like color, number of doors, length, width, etc. It may have methods like accelerate, brake, turn left, etc. An Object might be myCar. There are Class Diagrams that look like:

Car
Color String NumberDoors integer Length float Width float
Accelerate() Brake() TurnLeft()

I believe that the Object-Oriented paradigm is extremely useful, but is very difficult to teach to beginning students. I also believe that there is a lot of benefit in understanding how to develop and debug good solid methods before we get into the additional complexities of the Object-Oriented paradigm.

So there is a choice, we either teach our students multiple languages, or we find a way to teach them the basics of an object-oriented language, such as Java in a procedural fashion.

A few things that I will stress in this book are:

1. Good Coding habits. Writing code so that others can read it.
2. Good Design habits.
3. Testing your code while building it. I call this Write a little, Test a little.
4. Project life cycle.

I trust that this book will help in your understanding of Java and coding in general.

About the Author

Glen K. Blood has a B.A. in Mathematics from The Illinois Institute of Technology, a B.S. in Meteorology from the University of Utah, and an M.S. in Computer Science from West Chester University. He was a Captain in the USAF, where he fell in love with computers and the science and art of developing Computer software. He has held almost every role in software development including programmer, Systems Analyst, Project Manager, Team Lead, and Database Administrator. His experience has included multidimensional worldwide databases, orbital mechanics, image processing, product Quality Control, and marketing. Since his retirement from The Coca-Cola Company, he has been a part-time professor in Computer Science at the Coastal College of Georgia in Brunswick, GA

Chapter 1 Compilers

We have come a long way since the first days of teaching computers how to be useful. But languages and compilers are still complicated and need to be understood. The basic parts connect to the error messages that you get when you compile a program.

When I first started programming, you would submit your entire program as a card deck to the computer operator who would then load it into the computer, and then spit out a printout with your errors. You would then painstakingly go through this printout to try to uncover every error and fix your cards. Then, resubmit your fixed cards and hope for no errors. Repeat until finished. Sometimes, it would be hours between submitting your deck and receiving your printout due to the long lines of other students doing the same thing, so you spent a lot of time on each iteration.

Now you can code in an editor, run the file through the compiler, get your errors, and fix them, and try it again immediately. This is the real progress. This is why I advise writing part of your code, try compiling it, fix your errors, and test it. Then when you are happy with it, write some more. I call this process Write a Little, Test a Little.

This is as good a time as any for a brief discussion of compilers.

As we discussed in the introduction. Computers are stupid. They only understand zero and one.

Machine Language

The Computer Engineers that create a computer processor build in a set of instructions that are called **Machine Language.** Machine language consists of sets of numbers that directly reference registers, memory locations, instructions, etc. There are no letters involved. This is unique for each processor. Machine Language is executable code. In the simplest terms, processing looks like:

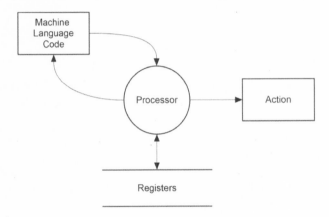

The processor gets instructions from the Machine Language Source, it interacts with its registers (very fast memory) and takes action based on those instructions and goes back for more instructions.

Assembly Language

It was felt that writing machine code was too hard for humans to understand, so the next generation was called **Assembly Language.** Assembly was a little better. Assembly instructions consisted of three or four letter mnemonics for the instructions and registers. Usually, memory locations still had to be addressed as numbers in hexadecimal. There was usually a one-to-one correspondence between assembler instructions and the Machine language instructions. So the Assembly language was still highly tied to the processor. You ran the assembly code through an Assembler to build the machine language (aka executable) code. This code then ran in the same fashion as described before. You still had one assembly language for each manufacturer (IBM, UNIVAC, etc.).

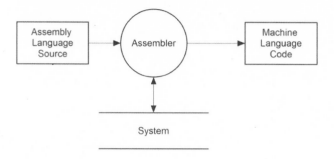

They finally got the idea that we could build languages that were almost human readable. I say almost because you still have to understand the vocabulary, grammar, and syntax of the language. These languages are termed third-generation. Some claim to be fourth generation, but I don't believe that any have broken out that far. Each of these languages have some form of Instructions, Variables, and Methods. They all allow you to combine many Machine language instructions into one simple statement. They all shield you from worrying about registers and the inner workings of the processors. Although some will let you to get involved at that depth (for performance). This has the following Benefits.

1. Languages tend to be transportable (to some degree) amongst systems. Unfortunately, some vendors built so many additions to languages (termed extensions) that even the source code was not transportable from one generation to the next for the same system.
2. Languages are much easier to learn.
3. Languages are much easier to maintain and modify. This does depend on the previous programmer. People can write unreadable (or as I like to call it write-once) code.

These languages generally fall into two types Compiled and
Interpreted.

Compiled Languages

Compiled languages, such as C, FORTRAN, Cobol, and C++ Take
the source code and run it through a compiler. The compiler takes
several passes and finally (assuming that there are no compile errors)
generates executable code. You have to build one compiler for each
processor.

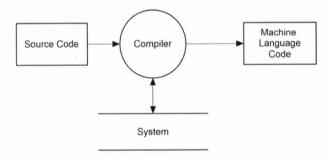

Interpreted Languages

Interpreted languages, such as Basic, take the source code and at run
time generate the executable code. Compile errors and run-time errors
are both detected at run time. This is almost (not quite) as though
each line of code is turned into machine code and run immediately.
What are the benefits? Interpreters give immediate feedback and
really came into use when the first micro-computers came into vogue.
The systems were very small and interpreters did not take very many
resources. Most of your Operating System command languages are
interpreted. Compilers are far better for batch processing (which is
what the original computers were designed to do), and give you an
idea of more of your errors at one time. Far better, they gave you a
clean bill of health (as far as compile errors) before you tried to run it

and they allowed the system to maintain the executable code separate from the source code.

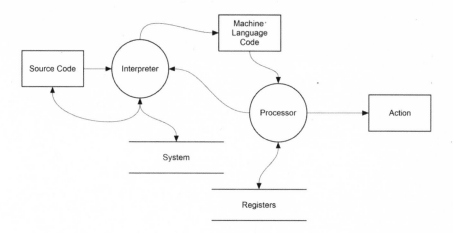

As you can see the interpreted process is very complicated and while not quite executing line by line, you can consider it to be that for simplicity.

> The interpreter takes a line of source code.
> Turns it into machine language.
> Machine language is then fed to the processor for action.
> Interpreter goes back for more source code.

Java

What is Java. Java has a compiler (javac), but that compiler does not generate executable code. Instead it generates java binary code that you have to run though the Java Interpreter (java). I would call this a Hybrid language. This gives it the following benefits:

1. Like a compiled language – most compile errors can be detected at compile time.

2. The Binary File can be maintained separately from the Source code.
3. The Binary File is "guaranteed" to be machine independent. So you can compile on a Windows machine and execute on a Mac.
4. It should run much faster than an interpreted language.

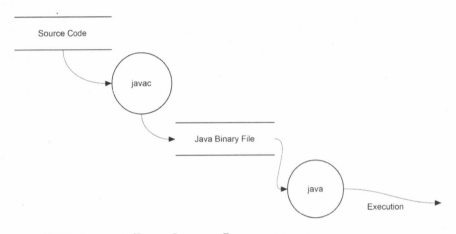

Steps to compile and run a Java program

Assuming that you have loaded the compiler into your machine or are using the class Windows flashdrive, and have setup up the PATH (to reach javac) and CLASSPATH (to reach the directory and import files) system variables correctly, you can run the compiler on your program file: ProgramName.java as

> ➤ javac ProgramName.java

The compiler statement either generates errors, or if error free, the file ProgramName.class. If there are no errors, then you can run the program

> ➤ java ProgramName

and it will display any output generated or generate run time errors.

Parts of a Compiler

Now let's have a brief discussion on how a Compiler turns your Source code into executable Machine Language, or in the case of javac, into Java Binary Code. This discussion will help you in your future efforts to debug programs. Understanding the parts of the compiler will help you see why:

1. One minor error generates many compiler errors.
2. Fixing one error seems to generate other errors.
3. Compilers will not find all of your logic errors.

The compiler consists of many parts. Each part has a function. And if the errors cause the portion of the compiler to lose track of where it is, it will quit reporting on errors or start generating bogus errors.

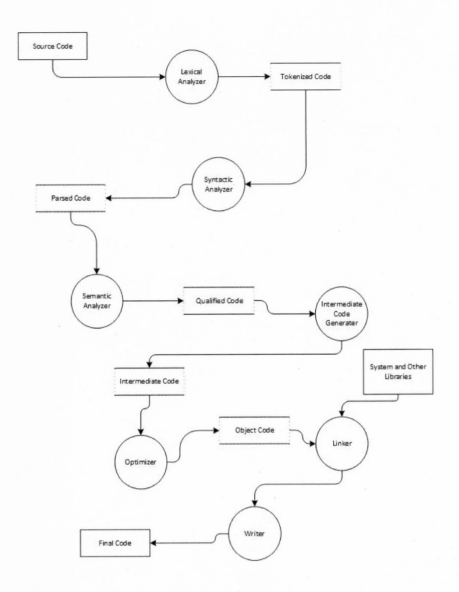

Lexical Analyzer (some discussions call this the Tokenizer; others combine this with the Syntactic Analyzer to call it the Parser).

Basically the Lexical Analyzer reads the code:
1. Removes comments
2. Takes every Variable, Constant, and Method name, etc and converts it into a token.
3. Converts numbers to internal form.
4. Identifies keywords.

Probable errors are anything that can cause it to lose track of what it is doing. For instance:

1. Paired symbols ("", {}, ())
   a. If you are missing the beginning symbol, then the lexical analyzer will try to scan all of the code as though it wasn't affected by the missing symbol, e.g., a missing double quote would be treated as though it wasn't a string with the expected hilarious results. Note: It usually knows when to expect a brace or parentheses, so it may actually give you a useful error. With code blocks (braces) it will give you unintelligent error messages.
   b. If you are missing the ending symbol, the lexical analyzer will keep searching until it finds any matching end symbol, e.g., anything after the beginning double quote will be treated as a string. Of course, everything after the second double quote, will not be, so then see (a). With Code blocks, it may tell you that it runs out of code to parse. With parentheses it may give you an understandable error message.
2. A messed up comment (//, /* */)
   a. Who knows what it will find in a missing comment symbol.
   b. In the case of a non-line comment how does it know when the comment ends?
3. Some bad syntax on expressions or assignment statements.
4. Missing semicolons.

Syntactic Analyzer. The next step would be to make sure to check your statements against the rules of the language, e.g., the Grammar. This step would make sure that: if statements, for loops, etc., make sense. I'm not sure, what exact errors would be generated, but I believe that these would be errors like:

1. Having an equivalence (==) instead of equals (=) in an assignment statement.
2. Missing semicolons.
3. Missing where clauses in do loops.
4. Miss-matching if /else groups.
5. Incorrect formats for Class or method headers.

Semantic Analyzer. The Lexical and Syntactic Analyzers only verify that the program consists of tokens arranged in a syntactically valid combination. Now we'll move forward to semantic analysis, where we delve even deeper to check whether they form a sensible set of instructions in the programming language. Note: This does not check into whether a reference may be defined elsewhere. Types of errors:

1. You do not define a variable correctly, e.g., you changed case on a variable name, or you forgot to define a variable.
2. You misused a variable type. You should have used String, when you used int.
3. You have code that can never be reached.

Intermediate code generator. This generates as much code as it can without external code libraries. It leaves place holders for external code. There probably aren't too many errors in this step, since theoretically most of the internal code errors have already been found.

Optimizer really depends on the system and language. Some can be quite sophisticated. Some can be very basic. They may go so far as to modify loops to make them more efficient or they may do nothing.

14

Linker. The linkage process goes out to the external libraries and fills in the place holders. There are several kinds of libraries:
1. Language Libraries
2. Company Libraries
3. Personal libraries
4. Operating System Libraries

Errors: Basically the only error is when it cannot find something. In java the error is:

Can't find Symbol - You are probably not importing the library or calling a method incorrectly.

Writer then writes out the final Executable File.

Java only differs from a standard compiler in a couple of ways. Since it does not generate an executable, and since it is machine independent, the biggest differences are in the Optimizer, the Linker, and the Writer.

The Optimizer does essentially nothing. All optimizations are in the system specific libraries.

The linker links everything except the Operating System Libraries. These are left for the Java Virtual Machine.

The Writer writes the Java Binary code or the .class files.

The Java Virtual machine (JVM) or java is much more efficient than a normal interpreter since the code is not source code. The code is already parsed, organized, and set up for the interpreter. All structures are set up so that it is not just read in line by line and turned into machine code. I do not pretend to understand the inner processing, but it is quite efficient.

Review

From the compiler standpoint, there are only a few types of languages:

- Machine
- Assembler
- Compiled
- Interpreted
- Hybrid

The parts of a compiler can be described as:

1. Lexical Analyzer
2. Syntactic Analyzer
3. Semantic Analyzer
4. Intermediate Code Generator
5. Optimizer
6. Linker
7. Writer

Most of your coding errors are going to crop up in the Lexical, Syntactic, and Semantic Analyzers. The Linker will show errors when it cannot find a reference. With Java, this will most likely occur because you do not have your personal libraries in your CLASSPATH or you have misspelled a method or class or you have forgotten to import a package.

Remember, the compiler can only detect errors in the language. It cannot detect errors in your thinking. These are also referred to as logic errors.

Questions

1. A compiler turns _____ code into _____ code.
2. An Assembler is used to turn Assembly Language into _____.
3. The Lexical Analyzer turns variable names into _____.
4. The _____ gets methods from libraries and adds them to your final code.
5. Java is a _____ language
   a. Machine
   b. Compiled
   c. Assembly
   d. Interpreted
   e. Hybrid
6. Most Operating System Command Languages are _____ languages.
   a. Machine
   b. Compiled
   c. Assembly
   d. Interpreted
   e. Hybrid
7. Without humans, computers understand
   a. English
   b. Machine Language
   c. Java
   d. Zero and One
   e. Basic
8. Most coding errors will show up in the
   a. Lexical Analyzer
   b. Syntactic Analyzer
   c. Semantic Analyzer
   d. All of the above
9. The Java compiler command is _____.
10. The Java Virtual Machine (JVM) is a/an _____.

Chapter 2. Java Naming Conventions and Components

Java has a number of components. Each component has a name. Unlike some languages the Java rules for naming are almost identical for all components.

Java Components

The components include (but are not limited to):

Packages - combine class files into groups for security, functionality, and distribution.

Classes and Objects – top level holders of other components.

Variables aka attributes. These hold values.

Methods – these hold code that do things.

Naming Rules

The naming rules are:

1. Start all names with a letter, dollar sign ($), or underscore (_). I would always use a letter to make code readable.
2. All subsequent characters can be any combination of Letters, numbers, dollar sign, or underscore.
3. All words are case sensitive. OneWord is not the same as oneword.
4. You may not use reserved words as your name, such as class, int, extends, etc. See Appendix B for a list of Java reserved words.
5. You should follow your organizations rules.
6. Make names meaningful.

I like to use nouns to name Variables, Classes, and Objects and verbs to name Methods.

There are two prevailing Naming conventions in most languages:

1. One called CamelCase, uses mashed words with the subsequent words capitalized. Sometimes the first word is capitalized sometimes not. This looks like:
   gearBox
   GearBox
   ChangeGears

2. The other called snake case, uses lower case letters and underscores to separate the letters.

   gear_box
   change_gears

Since snake case is mostly a holdover from c, and CamelCase is mostly used in Java, I will use the latter Naming convention.

Symbols

Your most common symbol is the semicolon ";". Every java statement must end with a semicolon. This is extremely important and ends up being the most common error. Another common error is adding a semicolon before you want one and ending up with a null or incomplete statement.

The basic paired code Symbols used in Java are parentheses (), braces {}, brackets [], and greater than/less than symbols<>. This is a brief definition of each, we will go into more definition later as we use them.

Parentheses () are used in several ways, besides in their normal math and logical methods, they are used to denote logical expressions and methods. For methods they are used to hold parameter lists.

Braces {} are used at the beginning and end of all code blocks. Including, but not limited to class templates, methods, if statements, and loops. I recommend placing a comment on the end brace tying the brace to the beginning brace. When we start debugging code, it is easy to lose track of which brace belongs to which and the compiler can quickly lose track when you are missing a brace.

Brackets [] are used for arrays.

Greater than/Less than Symbols <> are used to allow the compiler to know which types to limit certain classes to use. For instance, if the term <Integer> is used for a container definition then the compiler will only allow types Integer to fill the container. These are only used by the compiler.

Comments.

There are two sets of symbols used for comments.

// is used for line comments. Anything on the line following the // is a comment. Anything on that line before the // is not a comment.

The paired symbols /* and */ are a block comment that can encompass multiple lines. This is very useful for temporarily commenting out code. Notice that I said temporarily. In other words:

```
/*

Is a comment block

*/
```

As we will discover in our discussion of the compiler comments are tossed out during the parse phase of the compilation.

Java Components

Packages

We will not be building packages in this class. Java provides a number of packages in their libraries with useful statements. We will introduce them as we need them.

There is one package that is added automatically and does not need to be imported. This package is java.lang. For instance, String and System.out are two of the classes in java.lang.

However, in order for the Linker to find most of the packages, you need to include the import statement before the class statement in your code. For instance, if you wanted to use any class from the util package you would need to:

```
import java.util.*;
```

Notice that I use the * to enable the compiler to include any class from the util package. While you can specify specific classes from util, there is no benefit from specifying a specific one. The Linker will only include the ones it needs. It is not more efficient to specify the classes that you need. Therefore my recommendation is to always use the ".*".

I have included a package called CSCI for this set of courses to use. To use these classes, you need to:

```
import CSCI.*;
```

If you get the the "Can't find Symbol" error and it pertains to a method from a package probably means that you either:

1. Did not import the proper package.
2. Misspelled the method (look at case).
3. Have the wrong types on the argument list.
4. In the case of CSCI, you do not have the directory in the proper place, e.g., as a subdirectory under the directory where you are compiling your code.

See Appendix C for more information on package CSCI.

So how can you find out what packages you need? I like to use the internet. Another way to check classes is to use the javap command

➢ javap java.lang.String

which will give you all of the headers on all of the variables and methods of the class String.

22

Unfortunately, if you have the wrong package, you will get an error, so if you do not know the package, the internet works better.

One last hint about packages. The format java.util refers to a directory structure. The dot takes place of a directory symbol, so this would be java/util in one of your CLASSPATH directories or one of the standard java directories.

Class.

Everything other than the primitive types in Java is a Class or an Object. A class is a template. The class holds variables aka attributes and methods, including the main method. The object is an instantiation of the class. To instantiate a class is to bring it to life. You set aside memory and allow it to be used.

The format for your program class ClassName is:

```
public class ClassName{
} //end ClassName
```

Classes consist of:

1. Header
2. Constructor
   a. Method to initialize Object
   b. Same name as Class
   c. May or may not have attributes
3. Variables
4. Methods

Example

```
public class DisplayName{
}//end DisplayName
```

This program must be stored in a file by the name DispayName.java we will get into more details as we go.

Other Classes can be of two types, either static or non-static.

A non-static class must be stored in a file with the same name as the class. We will not be building non-static classes other than program classes in this course.

Static Classes are contained in classes. We will use these as Stamp Data types in this course.

When do you need to instantiate a class?

1. You should never instantiate your program or main class.
2. If a class has non-static variables or methods, it must be instantiated.

How do you instantiate a class? By using the keyword new. For instance, the CSCI class FileIn has non-static methods to read data from a File. It has two Constructors, one of which expects the Filename that it will read. Assuming that FileName is a String variable holding the filename, to instantiate a FileIn object Input, the code looks like:

```
FileIn Input = new FileIn(FileName);
```

FileIn does not have any available variables. (This is called information Hiding). It does have two methods. To read a line of data all you need to do is:

```
String dataLine;
dataLine = Input.Read();
```

Then when finished

```
Input.close();
```

24

If you have Static Variables or Methods, then you
without instantiating the object by addressing the (
to convert a string to an Integer you could use CSC
without instantiating the class.

```
myInt = CSCIConvert.Parse(dataLine,0);
```

Method

The main method is the initial starting point for a program. Every
program must have one and exactly one main method.

The main methods format is basically mandated. You don't need to
change it.

```
public static void main(String[] args ) {
} //end main
```

In fact the only thing that you can change is the term args. The
variable args[] is a short for arguments and is the string array of
command line arguments that you submit when you call the program.
The name args can be changed, but is traditional.

The rest of the code for your main method goes between the braces.

If methods belong to our current class then we run them by stating the
name and any parameters or variables that they need like:

```
MethodName(VariableName);
```

If they belong a different class then we use the dot notation like:

```
System.out.Println(AnyString);
```

So before we write any additional code, our first program looks like:

```
public class DisplayName{
    public static void main(String[] args ) {
```

```
    } //end main
    }//end DisplayName
```

This will compile, but will do nothing.

So let us add some simple code to it and compile and run it.

```
public class DisplayName{
    public static void main(String[] args ) {
        System.out.println("Glen K. Blood");
    } //end main
}//end DisplayName
```

System.out.println() is a library method to print a String variable to the screen. It automatically adds a return at the end. You will use this method all of the time.

"Glen K. Blood" is a hardcoded String. The double quotes ("") are used to enclose a String. You can change this to be your name.

Save this to our compilation directory as DisplayName.java

The name of the class must match the file name, including capitalization.

After you have set up the compiler, according to Appendix A (You will have to do this exercise every time you enter the command window.):

Type: **javac DisplayName.java** to build the java binary file

Type: **java DisplayName** to run the program

Glen K. Blood is displayed.

And you have run your first program.

We will get more into methods in a later chapter.

26

Variable

Variables have the following characteristics:

1. They have a name.
2. They have a Data Type (to be discussed in a later chapter).
3. They have a memory Location.
4. They can be changed in your program at runtime.

There are some basic types of class variables

Static variables – have a single copy of the variables for all objects instantiated from that class. You can think of these as Global variables. I would not use these for reasons that we will see later.

Non-static variables – not allowed in your program class. These are used in your class as variables. You will see how to define them in the Data Types Chapter. These are very useful in Stamp Data.

Constants – These use the keyword final. Usually the keywords final and static are used together. The only difference between constants and variables is that the value can only change when you modify and recompile the code. You cannot change constants at runtime. This is the only time that I would recommend (or condone) the regular use of static variables in your program. Constants are usually designated by using all capitals.

Writing Clean Readable Code

The basic Rules for writing clean readable code are very simple:

1. Comment well.
   a. Provide Headers to every class that explains what the class does. Explain the inputs and outputs. If there are tricks to the algorithms, explain the algorithms. If there are source books for the algorithms, you might cite your sources.

b. In your code explain your logic. Especially where the code is not self- documenting.
c. Avoid over commenting to the point where comments may be cumbersome to be maintained.
d. Avoid commenting out old unused code. Some companies encourage it as a practice to maintain versioning. Eventually, the commented out code is longer than the real code.
Personally I feel that it makes code very hard to read. If this is important, use versioning software to maintain old copies of the code. Or keep it long enough for some testing and then clean it up.
e. **important** Place a comment at the end of end braces to connect them to their beginning brace. Why? It is easy to lose track of which end brace belongs to which beginning brace. Example:

```
public static double
RecursiveFibonacci(int n){
        if (n < 2 ) return 1;
        return RecursiveFibonacci(n -1) +
RecursiveFibonacci(n - 2);
} // end RecursiveFibonacci
```

This ties the end brace to the method

2. Use Good naming conventions for all Objects, Variables, and Methods.
3. Use spacing and indentation.
4. Avoid programming tricks that produce really tight code unless you need them for performance. You (or your replacement) may not recognize them when revision is required. Remember, time constraints and pressure are always factors. I think of code written this way as write-once code. I have avoided mentioning such tricks in this text.
5. Be consistent. If you develop a set of techniques in your coding style, unless there is a good reason to change them, stick with them. There are several good reasons for this practice. Chances are you will make fewer mistakes, you can develop your personal library, code and tests, and your speed will increase. However, do not be afraid to learn something new.

Review

There are four basic components in Java

Packages - combine class files into groups for security, functionality, and distribution.
Classes and Objects – top level holders of other components.
Variables aka attributes. These hold values
Methods – these hold code that do things.

Java has a consistent set of rules for naming components. They basically boil down to:
1. Start all names with a letter, dollar sign ($), or underscore (_). I would always use a letter.
2. All subsequent characters can be any combination of letters, numbers, dollar sign, or underscore.
3. All words are case sensitive. OneWord is not the same as oneword.
4. You may not use reserved words as your name, such as class, int, extends, etc.
5. You should follow your organizations rules.
6. Make names meaningful.

There are some symbols recognized by the compiler. Some are paired symbols
"{}" – used for code blocks
"[]" – Used for arrays
"<>" used for type casting in collections.
"()" used for expressions, and method parameter lists
Some are specialized symbols such as mathematical symbols, * - /, and logical, && || !.

The comment Symbols "//" "/* */" are special.

Remember that the backslash "\" in a char or string is an escape character and has to be handled specially.

Variables have four characteristics

1. They have a name.
2. They have a Data Type.
3. They have a memory Location.
4. They can be changed in your program at runtime.

Constants (keyword final) have every characteristic that variables do except for #4, they cannot be changed.

We also gave some rules for writing good clean readable code. These included:

1. Comments
2. Spaces and indentation
3. Using good conventions and standards
4. Avoiding tricks.
5. Being Consistent.

Questions.

1. Objects are _____ classes
   a. Instantiated from
   b. Unrelated to
   c. Inherited from
   d. Used to define
2. Java Classes are not composed of:
   a. Headers
   b. Packages
   c. Constructors
   d. Variables
   e. Methods
3. Component Names may start with
   a. A letter or certain symbols
   b. Any alphanumeric
   c. Any number.
4. It is recommended that you use the following rules for naming except:
   a. Use meaningful names
   b. Follow your organizational rules.
   c. Limit yourself to six characters to make the names easy to type.
   d. Avoid Java reserve words.
   e. Maintain consistent capitalization.
5. Java Components include everything except:
   a. Variables
   b. Classes
   c. Objects
   d. Programs
   e. Methods
   f. Packages

6. Constants lack one feature of non-constant variables. Which one?
   a. They have a name
   b. They have a Data Type
   c. They have a memory Location.
   d. They can be changed in your program at runtime.
7. Which keyword is used to tell the linker to find a package?
   a. find
   b. import
   c. package
   d. goto
8. If you want to use the static method eat, for the class George. eat returns nothing. There are no parameters in eat. Which is the proper syntax?
   a. George.eat();
   b. George.execute(eat)
   c. eat()
   d. George myGeorge = new George(); myGeorge.eat();
9. Which method must appear in every program and denotes the starting point of the program?
   a. start();
   b. main();
   c. program();
   d. init();
10. When you use the keyword static in front of a variable in your class:
   a. One memory location is created and every object created from it shares that variable.
   b. It is a constant shared by every object created from it.
   c. It is a class variable and every object created from it has access to its own copy of it.

Problems

Compile, debug, and run these problems:

1. Modify the DisplayName program to display your own name.
2. Modify the DisplayName program to use args[0] to display any name. call it DisplayAnyName

Chapter 3 Data Types

Bits and Bytes

The computer processor and memory works in binary, or zero and one. These are referred to as bits. These bits are usually grouped in sets of eight bits or a byte. Most computers work in some number of bytes. The oldest microcomputers used 1 byte or 8 bits, later they graduated to 2 Bytes or 16 bits. Most computer processors and operating systems today can handle at least 32 or 64 bits. Windows comes in either of these two flavors. 64 bit Windows will support most programs built for the 32 bit Platform.

The memory in a computer has an address. This is usually denoted as a Hexadecimal (base 16) number with a range based on the number of bits that the operating System has. For instance, theoretically, a 32 bit Windows System can access 2^{32} addresses or 4 billion addresses (4 GB addresses). If each memory Location held 32 bits, then this system could theoretically hold 128 GB of memory. Since a 64 bit processor could theoretically hold 2^{64} addresses at 64 bits per address, you see how far this goes. Of course, this is only theoretical, they don't really access that much memory and besides you couldn't afford it.

Larger processors do allow you to access larger numbers for mathematical operations, which used to be a real issue.

Even given the binary system, computers by themselves could only understand unsigned integers.

Mathematicians, Computer Scientists, and Language developers have developed a systems of codes that map the unsigned integers to different data types. This allows these memory locations to be used as data. These are known as the basic data types. These basic data types are usually grouped into numeric, String, and Boolean. In Java code, these are called the Primitive data types.

Primitive Data Types

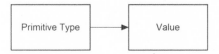

The name of a Primitive data type is its memory location and denotes the actual value. For instance, one of the basic types, is int (or 32 bit signed integer). To define a primitive type you give its type and name, for instance:

```
int Counter;
```

You can define more the one variable, as long as they are of the same type (I believe this can be less readable):

```
int Counter, Distance, GeoStationaryAngle;
```

Alternatively, you can set an initial value for the variable:

```
int Counter = 0;
```

The primitive data types are always passed by value. This means that when they are passed into a method, the value is copied into a new memory location. This second memory location is then used by the method. Any changes do not affect the calling routines variable. Therefore, when you return from the method, your original value is unchanged. We will discuss this in more detail later.

Java numeric values have two types signed integer (-x to x) and floating point. There are no unsigned integers in the primitive types.

Signed integers

Signed Integers only differ in the number of bits they use, which controls the range that they allow. If x represents the number of bits they use, then the formula for the range is: -2^{x-1} to $2^{x-1}-1$. The integer types are:

Bits	Name	Range
8	byte	-2^7 to 2^7-1
16	short	-2^{15} to $2^{15}-1$
32	int	-2^{31} to $2^{31}-1$
64	long	-2^{63} to $2^{63}-1$

So in Review, I would use int most of the time. Most computers are at least 32 bit and int gives you a large range of data. The Java Math libraries expect type int, and most of the time, your space requirements will not be tight enough to require you to use the smaller types.

I do want to caution you about integer division. Integer division only occurs when all elements in a division equation are integers. This is true of most programming languages. In this case the remainder or fractional portion is lost. It is not rounded, it is lost. So 99/100 = 0. There are programmatic uses for this, but only a few.

Floating Point Numbers.

There are no real numbers in the computer. There are only Floating point representations. These are 32 and 64-bit IEEE 754 standard floating point notation. You can think of them as scientific notation, but in binary. These numbers are not precise and you cannot directly control the number of decimals in our calculations.

How are they represented?

The numbers are separated into a sign bit(s), a Mantissa (m) and an exponent e (e). For informational purposes, the formula for float is:

$$(-1)^s x\ m\ x\ 2^{e-127}$$

The allows float to use 1 bit for the sign, 8 bits for the exponent, and 23 bits for the mantissa and gives you about 6 to 7 decimal point precision.

The formula for double is similar except that there are more bits available for the mantissa and exponent.

Which one should we use normally? I would suggest float, except that all of the Math library classes expect double. So I would recommend sticking to double, since you will need the math libraries at some point.

```
double PI = 3.14159;
double Radius;
```

String Data

Character Data (char). The basic type of String Data is Character. Characters are a single Alphanumeric, (A, B, C, …, 1, 2, 3…) and a number of non-character symbols (#, @, !, %...). Most computers use one of two codes for Character data. ASCII (**American Standard Code for Information Interchange)** or Unicode. Java uses Unicode which is a superset of ASCII. ASCII uses one byte to represent each number or character. Unicode uses two. While ASCII is pretty much limited to the English characters and some symbols, Unicode also gives you most of the international characters. To give you a rough idea of the encoding scheme:

Byte Value	Characters
48-57	0-9
65-90	A-Z
97-122	a-z

Unicode uses the same codes for these characters.

There are some interesting facts about the letter code values:

The Capital letters are exactly 32 less than their lower case equivalents.

They are numerically in order but case dependent ('a' < 'b', but 'a' > 'B').

The char datatype

```
char   mychar;
char Sex = 'M';
```

Character constants are denoted by a pair of single quotes , 'a'.

As a single variable char is not generally useful, unless you are playing individual parts of Strings.

Strings

Strings in any language are a collection of characters. There are several ways that these are implemented. Some languages, such as FORTRAN, do not define a separate String data Type.

There are three basic ways that languages define Strings.

1. As a character array with a pre-defined end character such as linefeed. The only issue with this method is that you have to use a special method to include this character within your array.
2. As a Character Array with Fixed Length. You define the length in your code. The extra length is then filled with blanks.
3. As a Character Array and an Integer length.

Java chose the third method. Java implements the String datatype as a class, but often treats it as a primitive value. While String is not exactly a Primitive variable, it is passed by Value. There are a number of ways to define a String.

```
String myString;
String myString = new String();
String myString = "Fred";
```

Strings are not stored like normal variables. Each String variable is not stored in its own location in memory. There is a String pool in memory. Each unique String is stored there. So if you have two String variables:

```
String Alpha = "Fred";
String Beta = "Fred";
```

Alpha and Beta's Strings do not point to different memory locations. There is only one memory location (in a String pool) that has "Fred" as a String. That memory location does not change. If you change Alpha or Beta a new memory location is created and a new string is built. And the variable is pointed to it. I have not been able to find out what happens when neither Alpha nor Beta point to "Fred", I assume that it is removed from the String Pool. For this reason, it is recommended that String is not used for variant Strings, but this is beyond the scope of this course.

One other limitation of Strings is that if you attempt to load a set of data into a String variable and that data has a linefeed embedded in it '\n', the string will stop loading at the linefeed. So if you plan to build a set of paragraphs, plan to use multiple Strings.

We will discuss String manipulation in a later chapter.

Boolean

Boolean data has two possible values (True, False) and is used in decision making. This is actually one of my favorite data types. If a language, such as FORTRAN or c, does not have one, I always built

Boolean constants, just to make code readable. Well, Java has a Boolean data type, called boolean.

Boolean data type. The Boolean type only has two possible values true, or false (lower case). I have been unable to find out any documentation on the storage size, so I assume that this is implementation/machine dependent.

```
boolean isTrue;
boolean ifthen = true;
boolean maybe = false;
```

Reference Data Types

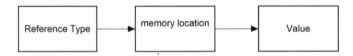

All other Data types are in Java are Reference Data Types. This means that they point to the memory location of the data. Not to the Value. This has a few repercussions.

1. When you pass them into a Method, you are passing by reference. Therefore, if you change the Value of the Variable within the routine, you will change the value of the variable when you return from the routine. If you do this without expecting it, this is called a side effect.
2. Your name is actually a pointer. We will get into pointers much later in the chapter. This means that when you use the assignment statement A = B or equivalence statement (A == B), you are actually exchanging and comparing addresses and not the Value. Be careful and use the appropriate method.

Stamp Data

It is often useful to combine the primitive data types into a single package. This is referred to as Stamp Data or User Defined Data Types (UDT) For instance, if you have an input or output data file, it is very useful to define a data type that holds all of the data in the record of that file. Let's say that we had a comma separated value (.csv) file with Name, height, and weight. That first few records might look like:

```
Kaden Diaz,65,242
Indigo Chaney,65,183
Harlan Hooper,71,200
Kato Mckinney,62,233
Rinah Norton,63,164
Eleanor Padilla,73,201
Quamar Ramos,66,177
```

While you could define three different variables:

```
String Name;
int Height;
int Weight;
```

Every time you wanted to pass this person, you would have to keep track of each of the three variables and make sure that they were in synch. Hence the usefulness of a UDT. This is one half of the meaning of Java Classes and Objects. This is the purpose that we will limit ourselves to in this class when we build them.

You can think of a Class as a Type Definition, or Template. An Object is the Variable or **instantiation**. Objects are always passed by reference. For this course, we will define classes in our main class. These are referred to as inner classes. Therefore inner Classes are defined in the following way:

```
public static class NameHeightWeight{
        public String Name;
        public int Height;
        public int Weight;
    } // end class NameHeightWeight
```

Defined within the class, but outside of the main, just like a method. Like class variables, I like to put inner classes at the beginning of the class structure.

You then define the objects like:

```
        NameHeightWeight aNHW = new
NameHeightWeight();
        NameHeightWeight bNHW = new
NameHeightWeight();
```

And you use them using the dot (.) notation.

```
// Load First Person
        aNHW.Name = " Kaden Diaz ";
        aNHW.Height = 65;
aNHW.Weight = 242;

        // Load Second Person
        bNHW.Name = " Kaden Diaz ";
        bNHW.Height = 65;
        bNHW.Weight = 183;
// Print out results

    System.out.println(aNHW.Name + " " + aNHW.Height +
" " + aNHW.Weight);
    System.out.println(bNHW.Name + " " + bNHW.Height +
" " + bNHW.Weight);
```

And your output is:

```
Kaden Diaz 65 242
Indigo Chaney 65 183
```

As you can see this can be very powerful.

System Types

There are so many system types that it is impossible to list. Like the UDTs, these are all classes. They include variables and methods. As we go through this course, I will introduce you to the ones that we will use. If you want to use more, you can ask or use the internet to research them. There are a couple of things you have to understand in order to use them.

1. Classes that we will use will come in two types utility (static) and non-utility (non-static).
    a. Utility classes hold a set of static methods (and constants) and do not need to be instantiated. In other words, you do not need to build an object to hold them. You use the method by stating the class name dot and method name. Example math.abs(mydouble) returns the absolute value of the double mydouble.
    b. Non-utility classes have to be instantiated into an object to be used. String is actually a built in class. So to build a Date object you would specify:

```
Date current_time = new Date();
```

2. Location. Each class belongs to a package. A package provides a secure convenient place to maintain them. Many of the classes that we use belong to Java.lang, e.g., Math, which is automatically imported. Other system classes belong to a package that has to be manually imported in our code: For example. Java.util holds ArrayList and Date. So to use either class you would need:

```
import java.util.*;
```

Above your class definition. While you can specify, import java.util.Date;, there is no advantage and you might be missing something else you need.

Course Defined Data Types

(The folder CSCI will have to be in your CLASSPATH)

While teaching these courses, I have built a series of static and non-static utilities in a package called CSCI which has been kept on the flashdrive. See Appendix A on the use of the flashdrive. You will need to place:

```
import CSCI.*;
```

With the other imports. And this will have to be in your CLASSPATH. Right now there are methods for getting a formatted current time, reading and writing and a Unicode string from/to a data file, checking for an integer or a double, changing a String to an integer or a double and other activities as needed.

Variable Security

You may see the words private or public proceed a variable name this is to define who can access that variable. Usually in class definitions variables are private and methods are public for information hiding. We will not worry about security in this class.

Static Variables

The keyword static makes a single copy of that variable for all objects created when you instantiate that class. This variable is a global variable for all objects of that class. If in the main, this makes it global for the entire program. This means that it can be changed anywhere at any time. This is bad news.

Except when you add the keyword final. Then this becomes a constant, as in:

```
final static int ERROR = 0;
```

Since this cannot be changed at runtime, this is useful and does not suffer from the risks of causing untraceable errors.

Review

There are two basic types in Java, primitive and reference. Primitive types point to the actual value. Reference types point to the memory location that holds the data. Primitive types are all predefined data types that are divided into Integer, Floating Point, Char, and Boolean. Integer and floating point are further divided into several types based on the number of bytes that hold the data. I recommend that you normally use:

```
int
double
boolean.
String (not exactly a Primitive data type),
```

Reference data types are the bulk of the data types. In Java they are all classes. Reference data types all pass by reference (hence the name) into methods. So if you change the value in the method, you change the value in the calling variable.

You can define your own reference data types. You can also use the built in System libraries. The system library classes include variables and methods.

Questions

1. We will be using the following recommended java datatypes in this course
   a. Alphanumeric, real, and Boolean
   b. String, int, double, and boolean
   c. Char, byte, float, and Long
   d. Numeric, String, and Boolean
   e. None of the above
2. The two normal ways that computers use to encode characters are _____ and _____.
3. Java primitive types are passed bt _____.
4. Most of java types are reference Types. This means that when you pass them into a method and change them without meaning to you can cause a _____ _____.
5. String variables are the only reference type that is passed by _____.
6. Which of the following is not a valid integer type definition:
   a. int Apple;
   b. int Apple = 1;
   c. int Apple, Orange;
   d. int Apple = 'a';
   e. int Apple = INTCONSTANT; // INCONSTANT is an int constant.
7. Which answer is incorrect about boolean data types?
   a. They help clarify code;
   b. The small size of the data type is efficient.
   c. They are a simple way to set an intermediate boolean expression value.
   d. They complete the data type set.
8. Stamp data is useful to:
   a. Group related data together
   b. Group random stuff together for convenience.
   c. Not useful at all.

9. Computer Real Numbers are:
   a. Imprecise floating point representations of real numbers.
   b. Precise representations.
   c. Valid decimal representations.
10. Integer Division type is defined by:
   a. Using the Integer Division symbol.
   b. Only using Integer variables or values in the division equation.

Problems

Compile, debug, and run these problems

1. Build a DisplayNumber program to display either an integer of floating point number.
2. Modify your DisplayNumber program to display PI from the java Math library.

Chapter 4 Methods

Note: Methods cannot be defined inside other meth
defined within the class definition, but outside other method
definitions.

Designing Methods

Methods have been around for a long time and ways to build good methods
have been discussed many times as well. Methods have had almost as many
names as there are programming languages. You will also hear those called
functions, modules, or procedures.

Methods serve several purposes in structured programming:

1. They allow you to break up code into smaller coherent chunks.
2. They allow you to reuse code.
3. They allow you to share code easily.
4. They allow you to test code separately.
5. They make code easier to read and understand.

The main design goal of a method is to build a black box. A black
box is an idea that has an almost identical relationship in physical
design. It is an object where the inputs and output are known, but the
internal workings are a mystery. The object can be swapped in and
out as needed without adversely affecting the workings of the rest of
the system.

In order to meet this goal, we introduce the terms, cohesion and
coupling.

Cohesion is the concept that a method has one purpose and its
independence from other methods. A method with one purpose is
thought to be one with high cohesion, one with more than one purpose
is thought to be of low cohesion. How can we tell if we have a

...od with high cohesion? A simple rule of thumb is to define the
...rpose of a method with one sentence. If that sentence cannot be
stated without using the terms "and" or "or" (or any related
conjunctives) you do not have a highly cohesive method.

Coupling is the concept of how any two modules communicate with
each other. Coupling ranges from loosely coupled to tightly coupled.
The goal here is to be loosely coupled (again think of the black box).
A loosely coupled pair of modules do not have to know anything
about each other to work together. It is much easier to trace the data
flow between modules. To test this module all you have to do is build
a driver program that fakes inputs and prints out the outputs. The
different levels of coupling are:

- Loose Coupling
    - Calling parameters (Primitive and Reference data
      types)
    - Function Returns (Primitive and Reference data types)
    - Messaging (Message Coupling)
    - Files (External Coupling).
- Tight Coupling
    - Global variables (static)
    - Content Coupling (Accessing the local data of another
      module)

**I would never use global variables or access the local data of
another method.** Global constants are fine, since they cannot
change. As I mention below I would restrict messaging and files to
specialized methods.

Methods can usually be grouped into one of several types:

> **Control methods** – These methods select from one or more
> options of program flow. Your main method is usually a
> control method. Unless it is your main, the option should be
> passed as a parameter or be based on the input (type of record
> in a file) and clearly defined.

50

Input/Output Methods – It is recommended that you build one method for each file/report/message queues you are reading/writing from to isolate any changes in format to that method.

Processing methods – These are known as business logic methods, and will be your major methods.

During development you will probably produce two other specialty methods.

Driver methods – These are small, usually main, methods built to test methods that cannot be tested otherwise. They usually consist of the minimum number of type definitions, print statements, and method calls needed to test your code.

Stubs – these are the first version I write of a new sub method. A stub consists of little more than the method header, a set of print statements to validate the input arguments, and a valid return statement. I then fill these in as I write and validate the rest of my methods.

Methods should usually:

1. Have one entrance and one exit.
2. Be short and clear.
3. Have a single purpose.

Method Header

Methods other than the main have a format very similar to the main

```
        public static Returntype MethodName(argument list
){
            Variable Definition
            code
} // end MethodName
```

All of the methods that are in our primary class will be static.

Most methods are of security type public. We will not talk about security in this class.

Returntype can be any single:

1. primitive or
2. reference type or
3. void.

If you have a return type other than void, then you must have a return (reserved word) statement within your method with values of the same type as your return type.

The return value is an excellent method of getting a value back from your method.

Note: For completeness there is one special method type that does not have a return type at all. This is called a **class constructor**. We will not be building these in this class. Constructors have the following characteristics:

1. They have the same name as their class.
2. They are used to initialize a class.
3. They have no return type.
4. They are non-static
5. They are invoked with the keyword new.

Your argument list consists of a set of variable type and name pairs separated by a comma. The argument list is used to pass values into a method, thus allowing you to use the same code on different values. In the case of reference data types, it is an additional method of getting information back from your method.

Your method name and argument list taken together must be unique within a class. The name and argument list is called a method signature. The return type is not part of the method signature. Its uniqueness lets the compiler define the method name within the class. This is how Java allows more than one method with the same name to be within the same class. This is called **Polymorphism**.

Argument Passing

Types can be either primitive or reference.

The names used are only meaningful to the method itself. You can call it using any name you want. Just ensure that the type is the same.

Header examples:

```
        public static boolean IsNotDouble(String
TestString)
```

isNotDouble has a returnType of Boolean, but takes a String Value

```
        public static int Parse(String InString, int
ErrorValue)
```

Parse has a return value of type int and takes two input values one String and the other int.

To call these, we need to define some variables:

```
final static int ERROR = 1;
String myString = "25";
boolean isTrue;
int number;
```

And Then we can call them as:

```
isTrue  =  IsNotDouble(myString);
number  =  Parse(myString,ERROR);
```

You can see that I did not use the same variable names when I called the methods, as I defined them. However, I did use the same data types.

You can pass arguments in two ways, by value (primitive data types and Strings) or by reference (reference data types).

Passing by value means that value of the variable is not changed when you return from your routine. You can change the value inside the routine all you want, but when you return it is not changed. For instance: Suppose you wrote the following code:

```
import CSCI.*;
public class TestPassbyValue
{
        final static int ERROR = 0;

        public static void main(String[] args ) {
        int input =
CSCIConvert.Parse(args[0],ERROR);
        System.out.println("Before passbyValue input
= " + input);
        passByValue(input);
        System.out.println("After passbyValue input
= " + input);
} //end main

public static void passByValue(int number){
        System.out.println("Entering passbyValue
number = " + number);
        number = number + 1;
        System.out.println("Leaving passbyValue
number = " + number);
} // end passByValue


} //end TestPassbyValue
```

If I run the program with an input of 5, It makes sense that that the first printouts say

```
Before passbyValue input = 5
Entering passbyValue number = 5
Leaving passbyValue number = 6
```

But why does input still equal 5 when number = 6?

```
After passbyValue input = 5
```

The variable input points to a different memory location than number. When a primitive value is passed into a method, a copy is made of that value and placed in a different memory location and is used by the method.

So how do you get the variables to change? This is the purpose of the return value. By setting a return type, and returning that value we can actually set a value into either the original or a different variable. This makes it easier to follow a variable's changes.

In this code the method looks very similar, all we are doing is changing the return type from void to int, and returning the modified Input. This changed program looks like:

```
import CSCI.*;
public class TestPassbyReturn
{
        final static int ERROR = 0;

        public static void main(String[] args ) {
        int input =
CSCIConvert.Parse(args[0],ERROR);
        System.out.println("Before passbyValue input
= " + input);
        input = passByReturn(input);
        System.out.println("After passbyValue input
= " + input);
} //end main

public static int passByReturn(int number){
        System.out.println("Entering passbyValue
number = " + number);
        number = number + 1;
        System.out.println("Leaving passbyValue
number = " + number);
        return number;
} // end passByReturn


} //end TestPassbyReturn
```

Now our output is:

```
Before passbyValue input = 5
Entering passbyValue number = 5
Leaving passbyValue number = 6
After passbyValue input = 6
```

By using the return type, we can change the input. However, while we can pass multiple values into a Method, we can only get one value out. Is there a different way?

The answer is reference types. Reference types are always passed by call by reference. This means that the actual memory location is passed. In our last chapter, we designed a stamp data type to hold three different data types. Let us define an even simpler one that holds a single integer, to allow us to see what pass by integer looks like:

```
public static class refint{
        public int number;
} // end refint
```

We are going to change our method to pass by reference.

```
import CSCI.*;
public class TestPassByRef
{
        final static int ERROR = 0;
        public static class refint{
             public int number;
        } // end refint

        public static void main(String[] args ) {
       //  Variable definitions

        refint refnumber = new refint();
        refnumber.number =
CSCIConvert.Parse(args[0],ERROR);
        //  code
        System.out.println("Before passbyRef number
= " + refnumber.number);
        passByRef(refnumber);
        System.out.println("After passbyRef number =
" + refnumber.number);

       } //end main

    public static void passByRef(refint input){
        System.out.println("Entering passByRef input
= " + input.number);
        input.number = input.number + 1;
        System.out.println("Entering passByRef input
= " + input.number);
        return;
       } // end passByRef

       } //end TestPassByRef
```

And the results are:

```
Before passbyRef number = 5
Entering passByRef input = 5
Entering passByRef input = 6
After passbyRef number = 6
```

Calling Other Methods

Methods can call other methods. In fact when we called System.out.println() we were calling the println() method from our Add methods and our main. We called passByValue, passByReturn and passByRef from the main.

Method Body

The Method Body consists of java statements and method calls. It is everything between the two braces {}. It usually ends with the return statement. We will get into this in subsequent chapters.

Review

Methods serve several purposes in structured programming:

1. They allow you to break up code into smaller coherent chunks.
2. They allow you to reuse code.
3. They allow you to share code easily.
4. They allow you to test code separately.
5. They make code easier to read and understand.

Methods should have high cohesion and be loosely coupled.

Methods should
1. Have one entrance and one exit.
2. Be short and clear
3. Have a single purpose

Methods should pass information through calling parameters or function returns and not global variables.

Pass by value means that a copy of the value is passed into the method and the calling variable is never changed.

Pass by reference means that the memory location is passed into the method and that the calling variable can be changed.

Primitive variables and Strings are always passed by value.

Other reference variables are always passed by reference.

The argument list in a method definition includes the data type and a name that is used in the method for each parameter. Each type and name is separated by a comma. The name is only valid for the internal method. You can call it using any name you want. Just ensure that the type is the same.

The return type is included for a return. The return type can include any of:

1. primitive or
2. reference type or
3. void.

If you have a return type other than void, you must have a return statement with a return variable of that type.

Methods can call other methods.

Methods can have the same name as long as they have a different argument list by type.

Method calls include a variable with the same type as the type needed by the method. You do not include the type and the name does not have to be the same.

Questions

1. Method Headers consist of everything except:
   a. Security Type
   b. Return Type
   c. Name
   d. Optional Argument List
   e. Parentheses
   f. Brackets
2. Method Argument lists consist of everything except
   a. Data Type
   b. Name
   c. Number of Arguments
   d. Comma separating argument pairs
3. Cohesion means
   a. How modules communicate between each other.
   b. How many things a module can do.
   c. How modules are compiled.
   d. How you set your comments.
4. Well defined methods have everything except:
   a. One Entrance
   b. One Exit
   c. One Purpose
   d. One Variable.
5. The Difference between Pass by Value and Pass by Reference is:
   a. Pass by value makes a copy of the variable. Pass by reference means that the memory location is passed.
   b. Pass by reference makes a copy of the variable. Pass by value means that the memory location is
   c. There is no difference.
6. Primitive Types and Strings are always
   a. Passed by Value
   b. Passed by Reference
   c. Can be passed either way.

7. Coupling means
    a. How modules communicate between each other.
    b. How many things a module can do.
    c. How modules are compiled.
    d. How you set your comments.
8. Methods consist of:
    a. Method Header
    b. Variable definitions
    c. Code or method body.
    d. Method declarations.
    e. All of the above
9. Methods cannot have:
    a. Different names and the same argument lists.
    b. Same name and the same argument list
    c. Same name and different argument lists.
    d. Different names and different argument lists.
10. Return Values can be:
    a. void
    b. int
    c. String
    d. Boolean
    e. Any defined Reference Type
    f. All of the above

Problems

Compile, debug, and run these problems

1. Build a Program called myMultiplier that
   a. Takes in two integers from the args[]
   b. Uses CSCIConvert.Pars(arge[i],0) to convert the args[i] to int.
   c. Call a method that you build called Mult(int X, int Y) to multiply these two numbers.
   d. Then Displays the two inputs and the result.
2. Build a Program called myDivision that
   a. Takes in two doubles from the args[]
   b. Sets up a double constant to 1.0 final static ERROR = 1.0;
   c. Uses CSCIConvert.Pars(arge[i],double) to convert the args[i] to double.
   d. Call a method that you build called double Div(double X, double Y) to multiply these two numbers.
   e. Then displays the two inputs and the result.

Chapter 5 Sequential Logic Structure

Basic Logic Structures

Now that we know about data and methods, we need to learn how to use them.

There are three basic logic structures in most programming languages they are sequential, decision, and loops.

We are going to go through the basic types of each in the next three chapters.

Sequential Logic Structure

The sequential logic Structure is the simplest logic structure and it is the one that is used in every other logic structure. It has three characteristics:

1. Beginning
2. End
3. Instructions that directly follow one another

Remember: Each java statement must end in a semicolon.

So what kind of instructions fit within this logic?

Type Declarations:

```
int anInt;
String Message;
String AString = "George Washington";
int anInt = 34;
```

64

```
boolean isTrue;
```

Assignment Statements:

```
myInteger  = 5;
adouble = 3.45 + myInteger;
aString = "George Washington";
```

Calls to Methods:

```
System.out.println("George Washington");
```

Sequential logic includes any type of statement that does not require the other two types of logic. You can actually write small simple methods or programs just using the sequential logic structure, but you will find that you can't do anything without it.

Assignment Statements

Assignment statements are extremely important to any program they are used to. In an assignment statement you place the value on the right hand side of the equals sign (=) into the memory location denoted by the variable of the left hand sign.

1. Assign a value to a primitive variable.
   ```
   Anint = 5;
   IsTrue = false;
   ```
2. Assign a memory location to a reference variable.
   ```
   myPerson = new Person();
   aString = "George Washington";
   ```
3. Move the result from an arithmetic expression, or logical expression, or a method, into a variable.
   ```
   adouble = 3.45 + myInteger;
   isTrue = (true || false);
   isTrue = CSCIMath.IsNotInt(InputVar);
   ```

Expressions

Expressions can be looked at as the left hand side or part of the left hand side of the assignment statement. They generally come in two types:

1. Arithmetic expressions
2. Logical expressions

Personally, I would make liberal use of parentheses to make certain that my meaning is clear. I would also break up large expressions, by assigning them to intermediate variables, to be certain that others understand what I am saying. Breaking up equations also helps in debugging, by allowing you to see intermediate values.

Arithmetic Expressions

An Arithmetic expression is an expression that returns a numeric value. The arithmetic operators that we will use are:

+	Additive operator (also used for String concatenation)
-	Subtraction operator
*	Multiplication operator
/	Division operator
%	Remainder operator

The order of precedence is the same as in basic mathematics:

parentheses (),
negation (-),
multiplication (*,/,%), and
addition (+, -).

You can logically put an arithmetic expression in any place that you would place a hard coded primitive variable of the same type. They never stand alone. Examples:

66

Alpha + Beta * 3.5 / Width
3 + 4
PI * R * R

Logic Expressions

Logic expressions are formed by a pair of parentheses "()" which
return a true or false. They never stand alone. They may be on one
side of an assignment statement or they may be in an if statement (see
chapter 6). Inside the parentheses is a boolean expression or equality
expressions or any combination of the two.

You can put a logic expression in any place that you would place a
boolean value.

There are three ways to express a logic expression (these can all be
combined).

Boolean Expressions

Boolean expressions consist of one or more boolean values, true, or
false, or variables (type boolean) connected by the boolean operators.
Unlike arithmetical expressions, boolean expressions must be
surrounded by parentheses (). The main operators are:

"&&" for AND
"||" for OR
! for NOT

(A && B) is true if A is true and B is true, otherwise it is
false.

(A || B) is true if either A is true or B is true.

!(A) is true if A is false and false if A is true.

The order of Operations is parentheses, NOT, and then left to right.

Equality Expressions

Equality expressions use the relative values of alphabetic, numeric values, or reference values to get a boolean value from them.

Note: primitive values are more straight forward than reference values. If you try using the operators on reference values (including Strings), you will be comparing the memory location and not the value, so don't do it. I will show you the right way to do it.

Non-boolean primitive Values

The operators are:

==	Equal to
!=	Not equal to
>	Greater than
>=	Greater than or equal to
<	Less than
<=	Less than or equal to

Assuming that A and B are of the same type (no guarantees if they aren't), The basic format is:

```
(A == B)
(A != B)
(A <= B)
(A >  B)
(A <  B)
(A <= B)
```

These are just expressions and not complete statements. Be careful and do not confuse equality (==) with assignment (=). Hopefully, the compiler will catch the issue, but I will not guarantee it.

One way to ensure that the compiler will catch your error is to reverse the normal way of writing an equality statement when you are using a single variable in an equivalence statement.

If you are trying to check whether the variable Counter equals 23, instead of writing it:

```
(Counter == 23)
```

Write it as:

```
(23 == Counter)
```

Since the compiler cannot put the value of counter into the literal constant 23, it will throw an error for (23 = Counter) at compile time. Thus avoiding countless hours of confusion and headache.

Note: Comparisons will work with char variables and there are times that this is very useful. However, you are comparing the codes and not the letters and it is case sensitive, since 'A' does not equal 'a'. So make sure that your characters are the same case or check bothe cases:

```
if (('M' == inChar) || ('m' == inChar))
system.out.println("male")
```

Reference Values

Strings and most reference values have built in comparison methods that should be used instead of the operators. These methods are:

```
.equals(a);
.compareTo(a);
```

Where you call the method from your object and a is another object of the same type.

.equals returns true if the values they hold are equivalent and false otherwise.
.compareTo returns an int denoting the relative value.

For instance, say you have three Strings:

```
String Alpha = "George";
String Beta = "George";
String Charlie = "Sam";
```

Alpha.equals(Beta) would return true
Beta.equals(Alpha) would return true
Charlie.equals(Alpha) would return false
Alpha.equals(Charlie) would return false

Alpha.compareTo(Beta) returns 0
Alpha.compareTo(Charlie) returns a number < 0
Charlie.compareTo(Alpha) returns a Number > 0

To use these functions, you would build an expression like:

```
(Alpha.equals(Beta))
(Alpha.compareTo(Beta) == 0)
(Alpha.compareTo(Beta)  <  0)
(Alpha.compareTo(Beta)  >  0)
```

Combining Expressions

Since logical expressions become boolean values, you can combine them using the boolean operators && and ||.

For instance; you could build an assignment

```
boolean Nonsense;
String Alpha;
```

```
String Beta;
int Height;
int Width;
boolean IsItTrue ;
IsItTrue = ((Alpha.compareTo(Beta)> 0) && (Height
> Width) || Nonsense);
```

Or it may be clearer to write the sequence as:

```
AlphavsBeta = (Alpha.compareTo(Beta)> 0)
HeightvsWidth = (Height > Width)
Combined = (AlphavsBeta && HeightvsWidth)
IsItTrue = Combined || Nonsense;
```

Which would let you check all of the intermediate values, if you run into problems.

Calls to Methods

To call a method simply use the method name followed by parentheses with variables in the same type and order as the method definition. The variable names in the calling sequence can differ from the method declaration. In the case of primitive and strings, you can substitute, hard coded values for variable names. Let us look at a few examples:

```
public static boolean IsNotInt(String test_string)
```

This method returns a boolean and is called with a String. It checks the String to see if it is an integer (a whole number), and returns true, if the input string is an integer, or false, if it is not.

Since there is only one String variable, you can call this in a couple of ways (assuming that isTrue and InputVar have been predefined and that we have set InputVar:

```
isTrue = CSCIConvert.IsNotInt(InputVar);
isTrue = CSCIConvert.IsNotInt("5");
```

Let us build a more complex method. One to print out how old someone is:

```
        public static void PrintPerson(String First,
String Last, int Age){
                String OutputString = " He is " + First +
" " + Last + " and he is " + Age + " years old";
                System.out.println(OutputString);
                return;
        } //end PrintPerson
```

You can call this with

```
        String One = "Uncle";
        String Two = "Charley";
        int  Age = 63;
        PrintPerson(One, Two, Age);
```

Or You can hard code these values

```
        PrintPerson("Uncle", "Charley", 63);
```

You realize that unless you mix up the data types or add or omit one, you will not get an error. For instance, while any of these will give you a compiler error:

```
        PrintPerson(One, Age, Two);
        PrintPerson (Age, One, Two);
        PrintPerson (One, One, Two);
        PrintPerson(One, Two, , Age, Output);
```

This will not:

```
        PrintPerson (Two, One, Age);
```

You will just have a Charley Uncle.

Another way to use methods is in an assignment statement. For example, in java.lang.Math, there are any number of math routines that require one or more double arguments and return a double as

72

a value. For instance, say you wanted to get the length of hypotenuse using the Pythagorean Theorem:

```
double A, B, C;
A = 4.0;
B = 3.0;
C = sqrt(A*A + B*B);
```

C is the hypotenuse of the triangle.

Putting it together.

Can we write a program using just sequential logic. Well, we already have. Your basic DisplayName program was a sequential logic program. Let us try something much more complicated. Let us combine a couple of things that we have learned so far and figure out the hypotenuse of a triangle:

1. We will use args[] from the input to keep from hard coding the two sides of the triangle.
2. We will use CSCIConvert.parse to change the inputs to integer.
3. We will set up constants for errors.
4. We will use sequential logic only.
5. We will use the java Math class to get the sgrt function.

```
import CSCI.*;
public class SequentialHypotenuse
{
/* 1.  args[] gives us the two sides of the
triangle.
     2.    use CSCIConvert.parse to change them to
integer.
     3.    Set up constants for errors.
     4.    Use sequential logic only.
     5.    Use the java Math class to get the sgrt
function.
     */
     final static int ERROR = 4;
```

```
public static void main(String[] args ) {
    // Variable definitions
    int Height = CSCIConvert.Parse(args[0],ERROR);
    int Length = CSCIConvert.Parse(args[1],ERROR);
    double HeightSquared;
    double LengthSquared;
    double Hypotenuse;

    // code

    HeightSquared = Height * Height;
    LengthSquared = Length * Length;
    Hypotenuse = Math.sqrt(HeightSquared +
                           LengthSquared);

    System.out.println("Triangle Height = " +
    Height + " Length = " + Length +
    " Hypotenuse = " + Hypotenuse);

    } //end main
    } //end SequentialHypotenuse
```

Possible results include:

```
::\java>java SequentialHypotenuse 3 4
Triangle Height = 3 Length = 4 Hypotenouse = 5.0

::\java>javac SequentialHypotenuse.java

::\java>java SequentialHypotenuse 4 5
Triangle Height = 4 Length = 5 Hypotenuse = 6.4031242374328485

::\java>java SequentialHypotenuse 4 4
Triangle Height = 4 Length = 4 Hypotenuse = 5.656854249492381

::\java>java SequentialHypotenuse a e
Triangle Height = 4 Length = 4 Hypotenuse = 5.656854249492381

::\java>java SequentialHypotenuse 3 4
Triangle Height = 3 Length = 4 Hypotenuse = 5.0
```

74

Review

There are three basic logic structures in most programming languages they are sequential, decision, and loops.

The sequential logic flow is not the most complex logic flow, it can be the simplest. However, you can do a lot with it. As you will see the other two depend on it, especially the logical expressions that we have shown you. Assignment statements and method calls will make up a considerable amount of your code.

The sequential logic structure consists of

- o Variable definitions

- o The Assignment Statement
  - Left Side = Variable
  - Middle = "="
  - Right Side
    - Variable or hard coded Value.
    - Arithmetic or logical Expression
    - Method Call
- o Method Call

Expressions
     Arithmetic expressions
     Logical expressions
          Boolean expression
          Equality expression
               Primitive
               Relational
          Combination

Questions

1. Which one is not a computer logic flow:
   a. Decision Logic
   b. Sequential Logic
   c. Random Logic
   d. Loop Logic
2. In an assignment statement, The Left Hand Side must be:
   a. A Variable
   b. A Logical Expression
   c. Blank
   d. An Arithmetic Expression
   e. A Constant.
3. A Boolean Expression must always be surrounded by:
   a. A forest
   b. Variables
   c. Braces {}
   d. Brackets []
   e. Parentheses ()
4. If A is True and B is False, then A && B is:
   a. True
   b. False
5. If A is True and B is False then A || B is:
   a. True
   b. False
6. If A = "eagle" and B = "giraffe" then:
   a. A.compareTo(B) > 0
   b. A.compareTo(B) == 0
   c. A.compareTo(B) < 0
7. Which is true about calling a method:
   a. It is important to keep the parameters in order.
   b. Doesn't matter what order you have the parameters in as long as you use the same names.
   c. If you have them in the wrong order the compiler will always tell you if make a mistake.

8. You can use a method call as:
   a. As a separate statement.
   b. In a logical expression.
   c. In an arithmetic Expression.
   d. All of the above.
9. What happens if you use the equivalence (==) operation with a reference Variable.
   a. It compares the Values
   b. It compares the memory locations.
   c. It gives you an error.
   d. Unknown.
10. You can always assign a logical expression to a boolean variable
    a. True
    b. False

Problems

Compile, debug, and run these problems

1. Build a Program called Differences that
   a. Takes in two integers from the args[]
   b. Uses CSCIConvert.Parse(args[i],0) to convert the args[i] to int.
   c. Uses an arithmetic Expression to display whether or not they are equivalent
   d. Displays the result of the first value minus the second one.
2. Build a Program the Calculates the Area of a Circle.
   a. Use Math.PI for PI
   b. import Radius from args[]
   c. Define a double constant of 0 to use CSCIConvert.Parse(String,double) to convert the args[] to a double.
   d. Area = PI * Radius * Radius

Chapter 6. Decision Logic

You make decisions every day, so why wouldn't a computer? After sequential logic the most used logic type is decision making. Decision logic in computer programs is used to accomplish many things, from setting values to changing the path that a computer program takes. Java has two basic forms of decision making statements (if else and switch).

If Else Logic

The basic form of the if statement is:

```
if (LogicalExpression) {
        code set a
} // end if
else {
        code set b
} // end else
```

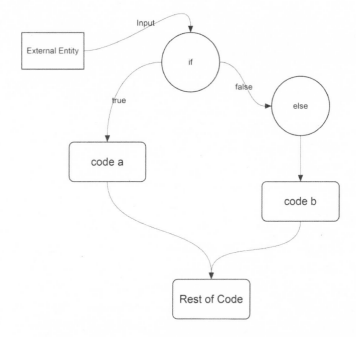

LogicalExpression is any logical expression (see chapter 5). The action statements go between the code braces. The else section is optional.

If LogicalExpression is True, then "code set a" would execute and "code set b" would be ignored. Execution would continue at the code block beginning after the //end else statement.

If LogicalExpression is False, then "code set a" would be ignored and "code set b" would execute. Execution would continue at the code block beginning after the //end else statement.

You can also eliminate the code block, if and only if, you have one statement, e.g.:

```
if (min > x) min = x;
```

However, I usually avoid doing this in case I want to add code to the if statement later. It is easier to add statements to an existing code block than to add a code block. Suppose you had a scoring program and were inputting one score at a time (poor design by the way). Scores were between 0 and 100, you might check the scores through an if else like:

```
if ((Score > 100) || (Score < 0)){
        System.out.println("Please input a
grade between 0 and 100 Score = " + Score );
        System.exit(0);
} //endif
else {
        ProcessScores(Score);
}  // end else
```

Note: For complex logical expressions, you can always pull your Logical expression out from your statement and substitute a Boolean variable. This allows you to test them separate from the Decision logic. For instance:

```
isTrue = (Score > 100) || (Score < 0));
if (isTrue){
        System.out.println("Please input a
grade between 0 and 100 Score = " + Score );
        System.exit(0);
} //endif
else {
        ProcessScores(Score);
}  // end else
```

Embedded If Then Logic

You can embed additional if statements entirely within either code block. They cannot overlap. The else goes with the if statement within that code block.

One word of warning, when building your expressions: It is easy to miss a value when you are using less than and greater than. So check all of your logic thoroughly and check the boundaries. For instance: Suppose you are checking ticket prices for admission:

80

Seniors 65 and Above $10
Children < 12 $ 7
Adults and Teens $15

One way to code this properly is:

```
import CSCI.*;
public class Tickets{
final static int SeniorPrice = 10;
final static int ChildrenPrice = 7;
final static int AdultTeenPrice = 15;
final static int SeniorMin = 65;
final static int ChildrenMax = 12;
final static int ERROR = 0;
  public static void main(String[] args ) {
  int Age = CSCIConvert.Parse(args[0],ERROR);
  int Price;
  if (Age > ChildrenMax) {
        if (Age >= SeniorMin) Price = SeniorPrice;
        else Price = AdultTeenPrice;
  } // Person is not a Child
  else Price = ChildrenPrice;

  System.out.println(" Cost of Ticket for Age "
                        + Age + " is " + Price );
  } //end main
} // end class Tickets
```

Suppose I slipped up and made Age >= ChildrenMax or Age > SeniorMin. Especially in the latter case, I would have some very angry seniors.

By the way, My Test cases for this included Ages (12, 13, 64, 65).

```
C:\java>java Tickets 23
 Cost of Ticket for Age 23 is 15

C:\java>java Tickets 10
 Cost of Ticket for Age 10 is 7

C:\java>java Tickets 65
 Cost of Ticket for Age 65 is 10

C:\java>java Tickets 12
 Cost of Ticket for Age 12 is 7

C:\java>java Tickets 64
 Cost of Ticket for Age 64 is 15

C:\java>java Tickets 13
 Cost of Ticket for Age 13 is 15

C:\java>java Tickets 17
 Cost of Ticket for Age 17 is 15
```

Embedded If Then Logic

You can embed additional if statements entirely within either code block. They cannot overlap. The else goes with the If statement within that code block.

Sequential Logic with if Logic.

One method of using If logic with unrelated conditions is to use sequential logic. These statements must be mutually exclusive. This can be identified in two ways:

1. The else is not present.
2. The logical expressions are not related.

For example, let us say that you sell hamburgers with three topping, ketchup, mustard and pickles. People can order them with any combination of the three (or none). Then your logic may look like:

```
if (Ketchup) AddKetchup();
if (Mustard) AddMustard();
if (Pickles) AddPickles();
```

Case or switch Statements

Case Statements are a way of simplifying embedded if else if statements. Unlike sequential if statements, they cannot be mutually exclusive. In Java they are only useful for an int, char, or String, variable. They are actually less useful than they first seem. You have to know, at compile time, exactly what cases you are going to need. The format is:

```
switch (SwitchVariable) {
case value1:
      step1;
      step2;
      break;
case value2:
      step1;
      step2;
      break;
default
      step1;
      step2;
      break;
} //end switch
```

Where

- switch is the switch keyword.
- SwitchVariable is a variable of type int, char, or String on which the cases depend.
- case is the case keyword.
- value1, value2, etc. are the individual case values of the same type as the SwitchVariable. (These are almost certainly hard coded or Constants).
- step1, step2 designate any valid java statement.
- break is the keyword that skips to the end of the switch statement, without it the next case is automatically executed whether it is valid or not. Do not forget the break statement.
- default is the keyword for any value that is not included in the cases.

Note: Although the standard allows the use of String, I would not recommend using String. I would not guarantee the results.

Example:

Where year is int and input.

```
String Grade;

switch (year){
        case 1:
                Grade = "Freshman";
                break;
        case 2:
                Grade = "Sophomore";
        case 3:
                Grade = "Junior";
                break;
        case 4:
                Grade = "Senior";
                break;
        default:
                Grade = "Does not compute";
                break;
        } // end Switch
```

This is equivalent to:

```
if (year == 1) Grade = "Freshman";
else
if (year == 2) Grade = "Sophomore";
        else
if (year == 3) Grade = "Junior";
                else
if (year == 4) Grade = "Senior";
                        else Grade = "Does not compute";
```

Obviously, you can use multiple statements or methods in place of the single statements in either if/else logic or switch statements.

Control Methods

One major class of method is called the control method. This type of method uses decision logic in determine which method to use. This is often done by way of an input data, termed a flag. In many cases, the main is little more than a setup and control method. For instance, suppose you were conducting a study that was based on the sex of the individual involved with a different set of steps for each sex. You might write a different method for each sex. The control method might look like:

```
public static void ControlMethod(char Sex){
    if ((Sex == 'M') || (Sex == 'm')){
        TestProcessMale();
    } //end if Male
    else if((Sex == 'F') || (Sex == 'f'))
    {
        TestProcessFemale();
    } // end else if Female
    else
    {
        ErrorProcess();
    } // end else Error
} //end ControlMethod
```

To Test this Method, you would need at least five cases. (M, m, F, f, and some other error character).

Final Thoughts

A few final thoughts on decision logic:

Decision logic code can become extremely unwieldy and complex, especially over time as additional requirements are added and expanded. Old ones are never removed even though they become obsolete and sometimes actually conflict. How do you combat this?

1. You can break up your logic into smaller pieces. If a decision is not related do not keep it in the same logic flow.
2. Break your logical expressions into assignment statements outside of your if/else statements. Use boolean variables.
3. Break the logic up into separate methods to simplify testing. Use control methods.
4. See if the logic can be rewritten to make it less cumbersome.
5. Ask for help.
6. If requirements conflict, alert your bosses and customers. They may not be aware that there are problems.

Testing

The only time to ensure that your logic flow is tested is during unit testing. This is where you can build test data that will test every branch and flow and especially the errors.

Review

So far, we have looked at sequential and decision logic. Decision logic is extremely powerful and complex. You need to be very careful and test all possible conditions. You need to consider improbable cases, and when you have multiple cases, for efficiency, you need to consider the likely hood of each case. You need to be very careful of a few things when writing decision logic:

1. Is it readable and maintainable?
2. Did I consider ever test possibility?
3. Did I ensure that I missed any possible cases?
4. Did I test my end and middle conditions?

The two main structures for Decision Logic in Java are:

1. if else
2. switch case

These structures depend on logical expressions which we discussed in the sequential logic chapter.

One of the main methods using this logic is the control method which is used to control your program.

Testing is critical of end and middle conditions are critical for decision logic. Unit testing is the best time to check your decision logic.

Questions

1. Logical Expressions are made up of:
    a. Boolean expressions
    b. Equality expressions
    c. Methods with boolean return types
    d. All of the above
2. In an if() statement what goes between the parentheses?
    a. Any int or char variable
    b. A logical expression
    c. An arithmetic expression
    d. None of the above
3. In a switch() statement what goes between the parentheses?
    a. Any int or char variable.
    b. A logical expression
    c. An arithmetic expression
    d. None of the above.
4. Where does the else statement go in sequential decision logic
    a. At the bottom
    b. Between each if statement
    c. Nowhere
5. What is a Control Method?
    a. A method that uses a flag variable and decision logic to decide which method or methods to execute.
    b. A method that has OCD issues.
    c. A method that operates a controller.
    d. A method that processes control data.
6. Which statement is true about a break in a case statement?
    a. It serves no purpose.
    b. It tells us when the case ends.
    c. Without it the code would automatically execute the next case.
7. In embedded if else statements the else belongs to
    a. The nearest if statement within the same code block.
    b. The top if.
    c. The last else.

8. What can you do if your decision logic gets too complex?
    a. Break it up into smaller pieces or modules
    b. Look at the logic and see if it can be rewritten
    c. Ask for help
    d. All of the above
9. What happens if you use a case statement with four possible situations and a fifth one enters, and you forgot to have a default condition?
    a. One of the first four runs at random.
    b. The first condition runs.
    c. The default condition runs.
    d. An error occurs – you get fired.
10. What happens if you use a case statement with four possible situations and a fifth one enters, and you had a default condition?
    a. One of the first four runs at random.
    b. The first condition runs.
    c. The default condition runs.
    d. An error occurs – you get fired.

Problems

Compile, debug, and run these problems

1. Build a program that finds out the type of the input data from the command line.
    a. Input is in args[0]
    b. Assume that Input can one of Integer, Double, or String.
    c. Use the CSCIConvert Class methods
        i. CSCIConvert.IsNotInt(String TestString)
        ii. CSCIConvert.IsNotDouble(String TestString)
    d. Print out the Results like
        i. You gave me an Integer = 5
        ii. You gave me a Double = 3.5
        iii. You gave me a String = Henry was a dog.
2. Build a program that accepts one of four letters – a-d and gives you the radio code. Use a case statement.   Consider that your user may use either case or give you some other letter.
    a. A = Alpha
    b. B = Bravo
    c. C = Charlie
    d. D = Delta.

Chapter 7. Looping

Looping is the last type of computing logic that we will look at. It uses decision logic and sequential logic, but adds the ability of code to repeat itself. Without this ability code, would be much longer, harder to understand, and take much longer to write and debug. Loops have three things in common and one major risk. The three commonalities are:

1. Start condition. Whatever condition they check must be initialized.
2. End condition. What breaks the loop.
3. Looping step.

The major risk in any loop is an infinite loop or a loop that never ends. You must ensure, when designing, coding, and testing a loop, that it has a valid end condition.

There are 4 basic Loop formations:
1. do while aka repeat until in other languages.
2. while loop
3. for aka do (not the same as a do while) aka counting loop.
4. recursion

While almost any loop can be simulated with any other loop they each serve a specific purpose or benefit.

Do While Loop.

do while loops have two basic characteristics.

1. The condition is always tested last.
2. The code is always executed at least once.

The format of a do while statement is:

```
do {
        code
} while (Logical Expression);
```

Where code consists of the statements that you want to accomplish.
Let us examine a code fragment that reads a set of integers from a file
and sums them. The end condition is denoted by the String constant
END. You have a method that reads a line of data and guarantees you
either an integer or the string "END" in order to denote the end of file.
You might write the do/while loop as:

```
do {
    InputString = ReadInput();
        if (!InputString.equalsIgnoreCase(END)) {
            NextInt = Integer.parseInt(InputString);
            Sum = Sum + NextInt;
        } // end if
    } while (!InputString.equalsIgnoreCase(END));
```

Note: Integer.parseInt() is a system method that will take a String and
turn it into an integer if it is a String representation of an integer. It
will throw an error if it is not. In ReadInput(), we have guaranteed,
that InputString is a "good" String.

WHILE Loop

The while Loop is similar to the do while loop. In fact, the two can
be switched back and forth with a minor fix to the logical expression.
The choice between the two is usually a matter of personal
preference: The while loop has three basic characteristics:

1. The condition is tested first.
2. The code may not be executed at all.
3. You may need a primer read to predefine the condition.

A primer read is an initial read of the data that allows you to set up the initial condition for the loop. This lets you place the next read at the end of the loop.

So the while Loop looks like:

```
while (Logical Expression) {
     code
}   // end while
```

And using a primer read, the same problem we discussed in the do while looks like:

```
InputString = ReadInput();
while (!InputString.equalsIgnoreCase(END)) {
     NextInt = Integer.parseInt(InputString);
     Sum = Sum + NextInt;
     InputString = ReadInput();
} // end while
```

As you can see there really isn't much difference between the two types of loops. They are both readable, they both accomplish the same thing, and the differences are very minor. In my opinion, it is a largely a matter of taste, comfort, style, or company standards, as to which loop one would use. However, I would be consistent in my choice once I make one.

for loops.

The main purpose of for loops is to increment or decrement for a variable. For loops need three things:

1. Initialization
2. End condition
3. Increment or decrement

The basic structure is

```
for (initialization; end condition; increment){
        code
} // end for
```

Say you wanted to sum from 1 to 10 by 1, you might write this as:

```
for( int i = 1;   i < 11;   ++1){
                sum = sum + i;
} // end for
```

There are several things to note:

1. The i variable is only valid within the for loop code block.
2. The loop runs from each value of i from 1 to 10.
3. The sum must be defined and initialized outside of the for loop.

Note: You can do a lot of tricks with the end condition and the increment, I feel that this is beyond this course, so I will not delve into these.

A final thought on these three types of loops. Any loop type can be used to simulate any other type. But, it is cleaner to use a for loop when you need an incrementing loop and a while or do while loop when you need a loop that has an unknown number of iterations.

Embedded Loops.

Just like decision logic, you can embed any kind of a loop completely within any other kind of loop. Note: I said completely. It has to reside within the code block. A couple of thoughts and or warnings.

1. The inner loop will execute once for every time the outer block executes. In other words, suppose your inner block executes 10 times each time it runs. And your outer block executes 20 times. Therefore, your inner block runs 20 * 10 = 200 times. So, if you

don't have efficient code inside this inner block, your program can drag.

2. If you make a mistake and do not initialize your variables, you can get weird results. Say you are dependent on a variable A starting at one in your inner loop and you do not initialize it and by the end of your loop it has the value of 10. The second time through it goes from 10 to 21, the third time from 21 to 32 and so on. Make sure you are getting the results that you desire.

Arrays

This is a great time to introduce a new data type, the array. Arrays are ordered groups of primitive (and String) variables. This is another example where a string data type acts like a primitive variable. Arrays are passed by reference. Arrays are denoted by the bracket pair []. Arrays are declared in two steps:
Step 1 declares the type:

```
Type[] name;
```

Examples:

```
int[] Ages;
double[] Weights;
string[]   Names;
```

The second step sets the maximum size of the array. This must be defined at compile time. The size can be defined by any integer constant, variable (within a method), or hardcoded number.

```
Name = new type[int];
```

Examples

```
final static int AGESIZE = 100;
Ages = new int[200];
```

```
Weights = new double[AGESIZE];
Names =  new string[1000];
```

Note in java: Arrays are base 0. Therefore, You start counting from Weights[0], not Weights[1]. You end at Weights[AGESIZE-1], not Weights[AGESIZE].

You will get an ArrayIndexOutofRange runtime error if you address the array at any point beyond AGESIZE-1.

Limitations of Arrays:

1. You cannot just add or remove elements to/from the middle of the array. You literally have to move the other elements to make empty space. This makes sorting expensive in either time or space, sometimes requiring a second copy of the array.
2. You cannot add space to an array during run time. Therefore, if you size an array for 100 elements and you have 101 elements, you will have a run time error. Therefore, you need to size your arrays for more growth than you expect to need and keep track of your data growth.
3. While you can have multiple dimension arrays, each array element must have the same data type. Therefore, if you have more than one data type, you must go through additional work which we will discuss in a later chapter.

Using Arrays

Using arrays is very straightforward.

Single dimensional arrays (we will get into multi-element arrays in a later chapter).

Setting values in arrays:

Usually, although this is not required, you start at zero and continue: sequentially. While arrays start at zero, you can address them from any place within their range and in any order. Since the array variable length denotes the maximum size of the array and not how many elements have been filled, it is generally a good idea to build a second variable to keep track of the currently used size of the array. Loading an array:

Single Elements:

```
Ages[2] = 34;
Weights[1] = 145;
Names[0] = "George";
```

Loop: Earlier we read in some integers from a file and summed them. Now, suppose we need to load them into an array. Since we do not know how much data we are going to load, the while (or do while) loop is perfect for this task.

```
InputString = ReadInput();
IntSize = 0;
while (!InputString.equalsIgnoreCase(END)) {
    NextInt = Integer.parseInt(InputString);
    IntArray[IntSize] = NextInt;
    IntSize = IntSize + 1;
    InputString = ReadInput();
} // end while
```

Notice a couple of things about this code.

1. We used a variable, IntSize to keep track of the placement within the array that the next integer needs to reside. IntSize can now be used to tell us how many elements are in the array.
2. IntSize was only incremented after the data was loaded into the IntArray. This is due to the fact that Java is base 0. So while there are one elements in the array, the first element is in IntArray[0].

Getting Values

Just like loading an array element, you use an integer value to get a value. You do have one additional condition, not only do you need to ensure that it is between 0 and the MAXSIZE -1, you need to make sure that it is in the range of the data that you have loaded. While, the system will not give you an error, you may end up with bogus results.

In the previous example we used IntSize to track the number of elements that we filled. It will not give you an error if you try to get a value that is greater than IntSize -1 and less than MAXSIZE - 1, but you will not get a valid value.

Assignment Statements

```
A = Ages[4];
B = Weights[i];
myName = Names[34];
```

Note: This is where the for loop shines. You usually know want to increment through the entire array, you know the size used, so you loop from 0 to one less than the size used by one.

Loop

```
Sum = 0;
for(int i = 0; i < IntSize; ++ i) {
      Sum = Sum +  IntArray[i];
} //endfor
System.out.println("Sum = " + Sum);
```

Using Arrays in Methods

Method declaration: Use the same form as the array declaration:

```
      public static returntype MethodName(type[]
arrayname){}
      public static double CalcAverage(int[] Numbers){}
```

Since you defined the array in the method header, you can use the array without redefining it inside the method. You do need to be careful that you do not attempt to address any elements that are beyond the maximum size of the array.

Method call: Just use the array name:

```
Response = MethodName(arrayname);
Answer = CalcAverage(Numbers);
```

Note: Arrays are a reference type so any changes to array values are reflected upon return from the array.

One word of caution. If you define an array inside a method, you can return the array in the return without defining the size outside the array. You may be better off returning the array in your parameter list and returning the actual size in your return. This way you can keep track of how many elements are used in your array.

Array Methods

Arrays have built in methods. You can find all of them by typing

➤ javap java.lang.Arrays

 in a windows command line. Two of the useful commands are sort() and binarySearch.

Suppose you had a String array, Books, a String Title, and an int Position:

To sort the Array, you would simply use the command:

```
Arrays.sort(Books);
```

Once you have sorted Books, you could use the binarySearch command to find the position of Title:

```
Position = Arrays.binarySearch(Books,Title);
```

Do not attempt this method unless the Books array has been sorted. By definition, binary search algorithms will not work unless the input data has been sorted.

Recursion

The fourth type of looping is recursion. Recursion is an interesting topic. On one hand it is a difficult idea to get across, on the other hand once you get the idea of recursion, it is very simple. Some people don't consider this a type of looping, but I do not see any other way to categorize it.

Recursion is defined as a method calling itself. The internal call uses a different parameter. There are many examples of recursion, and most recursive algorithms can also be done in an iterative manner. The iterative solution is often more efficient. The neatest thing about recursion is the elegance and simplicity of the solution. For recursion to work, you need two things:

1. An end condition to avoid the infinite loop.
2. A method call that defines the recursion.

A very simple example (and an efficient one) is factorials. A factorial N! is a mathematical formula used in statistics to determine the relative probability of a set of choices remaining after one has been removed. The basic example used is a baseball team. You start with 9 players, you choose the pitcher, which leaves 8 players. You select the catcher that leaves 7 players, until you are left with 1 player for right field. The formula is:

$$N! = N * (N-1) * (N-2) * ... 1$$

So the recursive code becomes:

```
public static double RecursiveFactorial(int n){
      if (n <= 1) return 1;
```

```
        return n * RecursiveFactorial(n - 1);
} // end RecursiveFactorial
```

And if you wanted to find out how many options you had to select your team, you call it from your main routine with:

```
NFactorial = RecursiveFactorial(9);
```

And it would quickly return 36,2880.

These numbers become very large very quickly which is why I chose double as my return code.

How does the recursive code work?

Let us assume an input of 4.

```
Call 1 RecursiveFactorial(4)

        4 is Larger than 1
        So it Runs 4 * RecursiveFactorial(3)

Call 2 RecursiveFactorial(3)
        3 is Larger than 1
        So it Runs 3 * RecursiveFactorial(2)

Call 3 RecursiveFactorial(2)
        2 is Larger than 1
        So it runs 2 * RecursiveFactorial(1)

Call 4 RecursiveFactorial(1)
        1 is not larger than 1 so it returns 1
        to Call 3
Call 3
        Return 2 * 1 to Call 2
Call 2
        Return 3 * 2 to Call 1
Call 1
        Return 4*6 to main

Main receives 24.
```

This is why this is called single threaded recursion.

As another example, Fibonacci numbers are double threaded recursion. The formula for Fibonacci numbers are:

$F(0) = 0$
$F(1) = 1$
$F(n) = n-1 + n-2$

Thus, the recursive algorithm is:

```
public static double RecursiveFibonacci(int n){
if (n < 1) return 0;
if (n < 2) return 1;
return RecursiveFibonacci(n -1) +
      RecursiveFibonacci(n - 2);
} // end RecursiveFibonacci
```

Since you have to go down the same calling sequence for each of the two paths in the   RecursiveFibonacci Sequence, this algorithm is much less efficient than the iterative solution. In fact, on my computer, while the iterative solution takes less than a second to return consistently, at an input of 45 the recursive solution takes about 7 seconds. At numbers not much higher, it refuses to return. Let us look at Fibonacci Recursion for a small Value, say 5. For Simplicity, our method is called RF().

F(5) calls RF(5) which calls R(4) + RF(3)

RF(4) calls RF(3) + RF(2)

RF(3) calls RF(2) + RF(1)

RF(2) returns 1

RF(1) returns 1

RF(3) = 1+1 returns 2

RF(2) second call returns 1

RF(4) = 2 + 1 returns 3

Meanwhile

RF(3) second call calls RF(2) + RF(1)
RF(2) third call Returns 1

RF(1) second call returns 1

RF(3) second call returns 1+1 returns 2

Finally RF(5) returns 3 + 2 = 5

RF(5) was called once.
RF(4) was called once.
RF(3) was called twice.
RF(2) was called 3 times.
RF(1) was called twice.

In an iterative solution. Each method call value would be called once and only once and the return value would be stored. Thus saving significant time.

It is often quite a bit cheaper, from a runtime perspective, to turn a recursive process into a non-recursive loop.

Review

This chapter concludes our discussion of the three forms of computer logic: sequential, decision, and looping. As you have seen, loop logic depends on both decision and sequential logic. Decision logic depends on sequential logic. Without all three we have long, cumbersome, unreadable code.

I introduced the four looping types and one new data type. The four looping types are:

1. do while
2. while
3. for
4. recursion

Most people probably would not include recursion as a type of looping and it does not have a code instruction in Java, but it is an important logic structure. If you become used to it, it has all of the attributes of a loop.

All loops have the following characteristics:

1. Start condition. Whatever condition they check must be initialized.
2. End condition. This breaks the loop.
3. Looping step.

The do while and while loops are extremely useful when you are faced with any situation where you need to loop through something until a situation changes. What they refer to as a state change. You do not know how many times you will loop, it could be zero, it could be once, it could be 10,000 times. Obviously, if you might never loop through it, don't choose the do while loop. In this class, you will usually use one of these two when loading data, since you have no idea how much data you have.

A for loop however is used when you know how many times and by what increment you want to go through something. Running through arrays, is an obvious use of the for loops.

Recursion is a method calling a method by the same name with different parameters. The loop ends by encountering an end condition within the method.

The biggest risk with loops are infinite loops which never terminate.

Arrays, while useful are limited in that they

1. Are limited to one primitive (or String) data type at a time.
2. Maximum size must be defined at compile Time.
3. Moving data in the array is expensive.

Arrays are
1. Base zero.
2. Can be addressed anywhere within range.
3. Passed by reference

Questions

1. Loops rely on
   a. Sequential logic
   b. Decision logic
   c. End conditions
   d. Looping step
   e. All of the above
2. Java Loops include all but
   a. do while
   b. repeat until
   c. for
   d. while
3. Java Arrays are:
   a. Base 0
   b. Base 1
   c. User defined
4. Java for loops require
   a. (variable declaration; end condition; increment)
   b. (increment; end condition; variable declaration)
   c. (variable declaration; increment; end condition)
   d. (end condition; variable declaration; increment)
5. One of the differences between do while loops and while loops is:
   a. while loops always execute once and do while loops may not execute their code.
   b. do while loops always execute once and while loops may not execute their code.
   c. There is no difference.
6. You cannot simulate any of the loops using any of the other loops:
   a. True
   b. False

7. Recursion consists of:
   a. A while loop calling a do while loop.
   b. A process calling itself until it encounters an end condition.
   c. A String function that reverses the letters in the string.
8. Array size can be defined using:
   a. Integer values
   b. Character values
   c. Floating point values
9. Arrays are passed:
   a. By reference.
   b. By value.
   c. You cannot pass them.
10. When you embed loops, you must make doubly sure that your:
   a. Variables are correctly initialized.
   b. Loops do not overlap.
   c. Logic is correct
   d. Inner loop is efficient.
   e. All of the above.

Problems

Compile, debug, and run these problems:

1. Build a program
    a. That accepts an input from args[0] and args[1] and converts them to positive integers A and B.
    b. Assume that your computer only has addition (no multiplication)
    c. Build a method to multiply A and B using a for loop and addition.
    d. Hint: Think of the way that you first learned to multiply.
2. Assuming that your flashdrive is on F:, Build a program that:
    a. Reads in the numbers from F:\data\numbers.txt
    b. Finds the max and min numbers
    c. Sums them and computes the average between the two.
    d. Hint: Get the filename from args[0]
    e. Hint: Use inString = Input.read(). This returns a String. When it reaches the end of flile, the string == null. You will have to instantiate Input as a FileIn object.

    ```
    FileIn Input = new FileIn(filename);
    ```

    f. Hint: use CSCIConvert.Parse(inString,ERROR). If ERROR is an int constant, Parse will convert your input strings to int.

Chapter 8. String Manipulation

We mentioned Strings earlier, but we really did not talk about how to manipulate them. Why? Well, we needed to know a few things first.

As we discussed in the chapter on data types, Strings are an array of char. They contain text. They are case sensitive. This section is on manipulating them, but, before we try to manipulate them, we might want to decide what we want to do to them. For example, consider:

String Problems

- Concatenation – putting two strings together.
- Separate strings at a certain character, maybe a comma.
- Find a given character within a string.
- Compare two strings – ignoring case differences.
- Compare two strings – but not ignoring case differences.
- Get a substring from a string.

Actually, there are as many different string manipulation tasks as there are programming problems, but many of them boil down to combinations of the ones above.

Not only are they an array of type char, Strings are also a Java Class. They actually contain a set of built in methods, that allow you to do things to them without writing code to actually accomplish those tasks. You can find these by typing:

> javap java.lang.String

String Methods

Some of these are:

```
int length();
boolean isEmpty();
void getChars(char[], int);
boolean equals(Object);
boolean equalsIgnoreCase(String);
int compareTo(String);
int compareToIgnoreCase(String);
int indexOf(String);
int indexOf(String, int);
String substring(int);
String concat(String);
String replace(char, char);
boolean matches(String);
boolean contains(CharSequence);
String replace(CharSequence, CharSequence);
String[] split(String);
String toLowerCase();
String toUpperCase();
String trim();
```

As you can see a lot of functionality is built in right there. (and I only included a partial list)

But how do you use them?

Concatenation

Which means, putting two strings together.

There are actually two methods:

```
String OutputString = First + " " + Last;
```

And

```
String OutputString = First.concat(" ");
OutputString = OutputString.concat(Last);
```

Example

```
String First = "Greg";
String Last = "Almond";
String wholeName = First + " " + Last;

Now wholeName contains "Greg Almond"
```

Separate strings at a certain character

For example, separate at a comma. backslash, period or any other symbol.

The method here depends on whether you want to find all of the substrings in a string that are separated by that symbol. Say you have a comma separated value (.csv) file. This is a common file type where fields are separated by a comma. The simplest way to do this is to use the split function to break your String into a String array.

```
String SYMBOL  = ",";
String SplitArray[];
Splitarray = InputString.split(SYMBOL);
```

Now SplitArray[0] has the first field up to the comma, SplitArray[1] has the second and so on.

If you had a file with a record structure consisting of name, height, and weight that looked like:

```
Kaden Diaz,65,242
Indigo Chaney,65,183
Harlan Hooper,71,200
Kato Mckinney,62,233
Rinah Norton,63,164
Eleanor Padilla,73,201
Quamar Ramos,66,177
```

You might write your record splitting code to look like:

```
String Name;
String  HeightString;
 String WeightString;
String SplitArray[];
Splitarray = InputString.split(SYMBOL);
Name = SplitArray[0];
HeightString = SplitArray[1];
WeightString = SplitArray[2];
```

The more common method of splitting Strings is using a combination of indexOf (some language call this position) and substring. The method indexOf finds a character or set of characters within a String. Substring, extracts a substring from a String.

Another common problem is finding the file names and or suffixes of a file. You have a couple of issues here.

1. Does your current filename have directory path included?
2. Does your filename have more than one period (.) in it.

Unfortunately, split does not like using the System.getProperty("file.separator") in Windows, since it is also the escape symbol. So we are going to take care of both issues in a very similar way.

Note: You want to use System.getProperty("file.separator") instead of hard coding the value ("\" or "/"), since this makes your code portable to Windows, Unix, or Apple machines.

Now to get from the complete filename to the full filename or the suffix, you need to use a combination of two methods.

```
int lastIndexOf(String);
```
and
```
String substring(int);
```

or

```
String substring(int, int);
```

Let us set SYMBOL to System.getProperty("file.separator") for we are trying to get the full filename and PERIOD to "." for when we need to get the partial filename or Suffix.

FileName.lastIndexOf(SYMBOL) gives you the integer position of the last file separator.

FileName.lastIndexOf(PERIOD) gives you the integer position of the last period.

First we want to break off the Full Filename, if PathFileName holds the complete filename including path:

```
FullFileName =
PathFilename.substring(Position+1,length);
```

Then the File name

```
FileName = FullFilename.substring(0,Position-1);
```

Suffix would be:

```
Suffix = FullFilename.substring(Position+1);
```

One of these two processes would work anytime you need to break a string into component parts or into a single part.

Find a given character within a string.

As you saw earlier, depending on what you want to do after you find it, indexOf() gives you the position, contains() lets you know that it exists.

Compare Strings

Compare two strings – ignoring case differences.
Compare two strings – but not ignoring case differences.

There are actually several approaches to compare Strings. The normal equivalence operator "==" sometimes works, but it actually compares the address of the memory location and not the string, so I would not recommend this approach.

If all you want to do is see if String A and String B are Equivalent, The method A.equals(B) works fine.

```
if (A.equals(B)) doSomething();
```

Which is equivalent to:

```
if (B.equals(A)) doSomething();
```

equals() returns true if they are equal (case sensitive), false if not. If you do not care about case sensitivity, then use equalsIgnoreCase

```
if (A. equalsIgnoreCase (B)) doSomething();
```

Since people do tend to be free and easy with capitals, it is quite common to use the IgnoreCase, when you are checking input from a user.

An alternative method uses the compareTo and the compareToIgnoreCase methods.

```
i = A.CompareTo(B)

A < B          i < 0
A == B         i == 0
A > B          i > 0
```

Maybe if you wanted to find the maximum string in an array strings. Let us assume that they are all upper case.

```
Max = "";
Length = StringArray.length();
for (int I = 0 ;   I < length; ++i){
      if (Max.compareTo(StringArray[i]) < 0)
            Max = StringArray[i];
}
```

Note: The way we compare Strings is actually the same way that we compare any two reference types, with the equals() and compareTo() methods. Strings (and their related classes) are the only types with the additional IgnoreCase methods.

Get a substring from a String.

For this you would use substring.

There are basically two versions

One lets you define a starting position and takes you to the end.

```
substring(int)
```

and the other you define a starting position and the length that you need.

```
substring(int, int)
```

As we saw earlier, you usually use these in conjunction with indexOf() to find your positions to start and end.

Some warnings.

1. You will probably need to experiment with various test cases to ensure that you are getting the substrings that you need.
2. You need to subtract 1 or add 1 to the indexOf() to omit the string that you searching for.
3. Substring does not modify the original string. You usually do not want to do this, there are replace methods. I have never had a requirement for them.

Last Resort

Although, I doubt that you will need to do this very often, you can convert a String to an array of char and manipulate the characters individually. You can then reconvert them into a String.

toCharArray() converts a String to a char array.

This code reverses a String

```
myChars = Input.toCharArray();
Size = Input.length();
Reverse = "";
for(int i = Size-1; i >=0; --i){
      Reverse = Reverse + myChars[i];
}//end for
```

This code converts a char array to a String. Assume that myChars is your array and Size, the used size of that character array.

```
String newString = "";
for (int i = 0; i < Size; ++i){
      newString = newString + myChars[i];
  }
```

Review

Strings are a special datatype. They are a reference data type that acts like a primitive type. They are passed by value. They can be used in arrays, Unlike every other data type that I know of, they share a data space that holds every unique string. When a new String is added the String variable is pointed to that unique string. When an existing String is changed, a new string is added to that data space. If two String variables are identical, then they point to that same memory location (most of the time – no guarantee). However, a String Literal may not.

Strings have a lot of built in functionality (methods) that will handle most of the manipulation that you will need to do to them.

It is recommended that you use equals() and compareTo() for comparisons. Because of case sensitivity and the lack of care that most people have when entering data it is actually recommended that you usually use equalsIgnoreCase() and compareToIgnoreCase() unless case is necessary.

The split(), IndexOf(), and substring() methods are extremely useful for breaking up strings on known symbols. This is a very common exercise when manipulating data.

When nothing else will work it is always possible to break up the String into a char array and manipulate it that way. This is not recommended, but mentioned as a last resort.

Questions

1. Which statement is untrue about Strings:
   a. They are arrays of Characters
   b. They are a primitive type
   c. They have built in methods
   d. They are a reference type that acts like a primitive type.
2. You have to worry about System.getProperty("file.separator") because:
   a. In Windows the file separator is also the escape character
   b. It is not always initialized.
   c. You have to import the util library to get the system class.
   d. You do not need to worry about it.
3. You might use indexOf() and substring() together because:
   a. It confuses the heck out of people
   b. indexOf() gives you the position of the character on which to break your string and substring() does the break.
   c. substring() gives you the position of the character on which to break your string and indexOf() does the break.
   d. indexOf() tells you how many strings you end up with in your string array when you use your substring() method.
4. The split() method is very useful when:
   a. You are trying to find a substring.
   b. You have a large file to break into smaller chunks.
   c. You have assets to separate in a divorce settlement.
   d. You are trying to decode a character delimitated record.
5. Why don't you want to use the standard comparison symbols (==) to check equivalence for strings?
   a. They never work.
   b. They actually check memory locations and not Value.
   c. It is too easy and we like to make it harder on you.
   d. It is too hard to understand.

6. Why would you want to split Strings into char Arrays and manipulate them?
   a. It is much less complicated and makes for cleaner code than using the built in methods.
   b. It is much more efficient than the built in libraries.
   c. Some rare things are cleaner than trying to make the built in methods fit.
   d. We are stubborn.
7. Why would you want to use the equalsIgnoreCase and compareToIgnoreCase case options?
   a. People are lazy and do not follow their own case rules.
   b. You don't. Always follow case.
   c. Change all of your data to either upper or lower case.
   d. There are times when either case is valid.
   e. a and d.
8. When you pass a String into a method and change the value of that String within the method, the:
   a. Value of the String outside the method changes.
   b. Value of the String outside the method is unchanged.
   c. Program blows up.
9. When two Strings have identical information:
   a. They always have their own unique memory location.
   b. They probably share the same memory location in the string space.
   c. They are the same variable.
10. When a String is changed
    a. The String in the String space is changed.
    b. A new String is created in the String space and the old String is deleted.
    c. A new String is created in the String space and it is unknown what happens to the old one.

Problems

Compile, debug, and run these problems

1. Write a program that accepts two strings from args[0] and args[1]
    into A and B
    a. Find the first position of A in B. Case independent.
    b. Remove A from B and put it into a Third String C.
    c. Display A, B, and C
    d. Example: if Cat and Meercat were the inputs. Then Cat,
        Meercat and Meer would be the outputs.
    e. Hint: I would probably copy the original strings into
        intermediate variables and make them both the same case
        for manipulation.
2. Write a program that finds out if an input strings args[0] is a
    palindrome:
    a. A palindrome is a word or phrase that is spelled the same
        forwards and backwards.
    b. Ignore capitals, special characters, and spaces.

3. Write a program that reads in the file names.txt from data\ on the
    flashdrive and counts all of the unique first names in the file. Find
    the name that occurs the most.
    a. Note: you will want to import the filename as args[0] to
        avoid hardcoding the filename.

Chapter 9. Advanced Data Types

Multidimensional Arrays

Two dimensional Arrays.

When you look at a spreadsheet, you see rows and columns. You
sometimes want to do the same thing in code. You can build an array
with two dimensions. The format for an array with two dimensions is
similar to a one-dimensional array, using two sets of brackets:

```
type[][] myArray = new type[Columns][Rows];
```

Where: Rows and Columns are constants of type int and type is any
Primitive type or String.

What can you use it for?

Anytime you have data that is of the same type that you want to keep
together, multidimensional arrays work very nicely. When data is
not of the same type, there are other methods.

How do you use it? Perhaps a couple of examples would let you see
this.

Example 1. Remember our Radio Alphabet. We had two variables, Letter and Code. Suppose, we read in each as String from a file (for simplicity, we will assume that our file only has good data). Assuming that all constants, variables, and objects have been defined:

```
String[][] RadioAlphabet =
new String[2][AlPHASIZE];
inputString = RadioFile.Read();
while (inputString !=null){
     SplitString = inputString.split(COMMA);
     RadioAlphabet[0][Size] = SplitString[0];
     RadioAlphabet[1][Size] = SplitString[1];
     ++Size;
     inputString = RadioFile.Read();
} // end While
```

Notice, that we are using the same split method that we encountered in the previous chapter, but we are putting the zero member, letter, into the zero member of our radio file array. We are then putting the one member, radio code, into the one member of our radio file array. This keeps things nice and tidy.

Note: I often declare constants for zero, say LETTER, and one, say CODE, in this case to make it clear which member of the array would mean which value.

You can now set up a menu and allow your user to input a letter and display the related code. To display the entire array, I would use a simple for loop:

```
for (int i = 0; i < Size; ++i ){
     System.out.println(RadioAlphabet[0][i]
+ " = " + RadioAlphabet[1][i]);
}
```

Example 2. Suppose we have a .csv file with heights and weights and your boss wants you to load an array and compute BMI. The input data looks like:

```
68,206
71,127
71,241
72,152
```

Note: BMI = (Weight in Pounds / (Height in inches x Height in inches)) x 703

We define a two dimension Array with FMAXSIZE (a constant larger than the expected size of the file, as the expected size. The Array holds height in element [0] and weight in [1] of each row.

```
int[][]  HeightWeight = new [2][FMAXSIZE];
```

We also need a datatype to denote a single record. This would be one dimensional two element array of height and weight. We state that if height or element [0] == 0, then the record is empty.

Note: We are using constants HEIGHT (0) and WEIGHT (1) to make the code more readable. This way, you do not have to remember which column is which value.

```
int[] HW = new int[2];
```

So the code to load the file into our array looks like:

```
HWSize = 0;
HW = ReadHeightWeightRecord(HeightFile);
while(HW[HEIGHT] > 0) {

     HeightWeight[HEIGHT] [HWSize] = HW[HEIGHT];
     HeightWeight[WEIGHT] [HWSize] = HW[WEIGHT];
     ++HWSize;
     HW = ReadHeightWeightRecord(HeightFile);
} // end While
```

Note: while we could make HeightWeight[HWSize] = HW work as a shortcut, this copies the memory location of HW into the position of HeightWeight[HWSize] and is probably not the best way to do it, especially if you do not create HW as a new memory location each time.

To use this data, we simply need a for loop. I pulled the data out into separate variables, just to make it easier to read:

```
for (int i = 0; i < HWSize; ++i){
   Height = HeightWeight[HEIGHT][i];
   Weight = HeightWeight[WEIGHT][i];
   BMI = ( Weight/( Height * Height  ) ) * 703 ;
   outputline = "Height = " + Height
+ " Weight = " + Weight + " BMI = " + BMI ;
      System.out.println (outputline);
} // end for
```

It is permissible to build more dimensions with the same methods and the same limitations. The worst limitation is that they have to have the same data type. One unique thing about Java is that the final dimension can vary in size. In other words, it does not have to have a fixed size. However, this is beyond the scope of this class.

Mixed Data Types

As we have seen, two dimensional arrays or multi-dimensional arrays are limited to the same data type. In real life we are rarely limited to the same data type. We usually we want to mix up data types. There are a number of ways to handle this. We will explore three of the more obvious ones.

Say we have an additional column in the data that we had in the previous section, name. It would be useful, one might say crucial, to know who our weights and heights belonged to: So our data now looks like:

```
Kaden Diaz,65,242
Indigo Chaney,65,183
Harlan Hooper,71,200
Kato Mckinney,62,233
Rinah Norton,63,164
Eleanor Padilla,73,201
Quamar Ramos,66,177
```

Data Structures are a term for a way to store data. We are going to look at several different data structures that can be used to solve this problem. We will look at three code snippets from each to see some of the differences in complexities. These code snippets are loading the data, using the data (calculating BMI and printing it) and performing an insertion sort.

Solution 1. String Arrays

Can we build a two dimensional array with three columns? Arrays have to have the same data type. In our example, we have two data types, string and integer. We could leave the two integer columns as string and have a three column String array.

```
String [] NameHeightWeight =
        new String[3][FMAXSIZE]
```

Of course we would want to make sure that they were integer when we read in the data and then we would have to convert the two other columns whenever we want to use them. This has a processing cost and adds to code complexity. If we defined a new Constant NAME with a value of three.

```
NameHeightWeight[NAME][2] = "Harlan Hooper"
NameHeightWeight[HEIGHT][2] = "71"
NameHeightWeight[WEIGHT][2] = "200"
```

We already have methods in CSCIConvert.IsNotInt(String) for testing integer, so adding logic like:

```
if(CSCIConvert.IsNotInt(weightString)){
        HW[WEIGHT] = ERRORSTRING;
}
else {
        HW(WEIGHT] = weightString;
}
```

To Load the data, Since all of the data is String when it enters the system, this code is very straightforward:

```
Record = readRecord(Input);
while(Record[1].compareTo("0") > 0) {
        NameHeightWeight[HEIGHT][Size] =
        Record[1];
        NameHeightWeight[WEIGHT][Size] =
        Record[2];
        NameHeightWeight[NAME][Size] = Record[0];
        ++Size;
        Record = readRecord(Input);
} // end While
```

Using the Data. To compute BMI, you have to convert Height and Weight to integer. You already are guaranteed that the values are integer.

```
for (int i = 0; i < Size; ++i){
        Name = NameHeightWeight[NAME][i];
        Height = NameHeightWeight[HEIGHT][i];
        Weight = NameHeightWeight[WEIGHT][i];
        iHeight = convert(Height);
        iWeight = convert(Weight);
        BMI = computeBMI(iHeight,iWeight);
        outLine =
String.format(FORMATSTRING,Name,Height,Weight,BMI);
        System.out.println(outLine);
    }
```

Insertion sort. The only complexity here is the fact that all three columns have to be moved.

```
for(int i = 1; i < size; i++) {
j = i - 1;
      temp[NAME] = A[NAME][i];
      temp[HEIGHT] = A[HEIGHT][i];
      temp[WEIGHT] = A[WEIGHT][i];
      while(j >= 0 && (
      temp[NAME].compareToIgnoreCase(A[NAME][j])
      < 0)) {
            A[NAME][j + 1] = A[NAME][j];
            A[HEIGHT][j + 1] = A[HEIGHT][j];
            A[WEIGHT][j + 1] = A[WEIGHT][j];
            --j;
      }
      A[NAME][j + 1] = temp[NAME];
      A[HEIGHT][j + 1] = temp[HEIGHT];
      A[WEIGHT][j + 1] = temp[WEIGHT];
}
```

Solution 2 Parallel Arrays

Another solution is called Parallel Arrays. Parallel arrays are separate arrays that are kept synchronized (or in parallel). In other words, the data in the ith row in one array is related to the ith row in each of the other arrays. Loading the data.

So we could have either three one-dimensional arrays or one one-dimensional array and the same two-dimensional array as the last problem. Say we chose the latter solution.

```
String[] Names = new String[FMAXSIZE]
int[][]  HeightWeight = new int [2][FMAXSIZE];
```

based on the data above

```
Names[2] = "Harlan Hooper"
HeightWeight[2][HEIGHT] = 71
HeightWeight[2][WEIGHT] = 200
```

The biggest drawback to this solution is if you need to sort one array, say name, you have to keep the other two arrays in synch.

There are three main code snippet types that we can see

For simplicity, let's leave the ReadHeightWeightRecord(String) to return a String array with name, height and weight as in the previous example.

We will only need to convert the data once. So our read routine now looks like:

```
Record = readRecord(Input);
while(Record[1].compareTo("0") > 0) {
        HeightWeight[HEIGHT][Size] =
        convert(Record[1]);
        HeightWeight[WEIGHT][Size] =
        convert(Record[2]);
        Names[Size] = Record[0];
        ++Size;
        Record = readRecord(Input);
} // end While
```

To use the data, we no longer need to convert the height and weight.

```
for (int i = 0; i < Size; ++i){
        Name = Names[i];
        iHeight = HeightWeight[HEIGHT][i];
        iWeight = HeightWeight[WEIGHT][i];
        BMI = computeBMI(iHeight,iWeight);
        outLine =
String.format(FORMATSTRING,Name,iHeight,iWeight
,BMI);
        System.out.println(outLine);
}
```

To perform an insertion, sort. We still need to keep the two arrays in synch, so both arrays, need to participate in the sort.

```
for(int i = 1; i < size; i++) {
    j = i - 1;
    temp = A[i];
    tempi[HEIGHT] = B[HEIGHT][i];
    tempi[WEIGHT] = B[WEIGHT][i];
    while(j >= 0 &&
    (temp.compareToIgnoreCase(A[j]) < 0)) {
        A[j + 1] = A[j];
        B[HEIGHT][j + 1] = B[HEIGHT][j];
        B[WEIGHT][j + 1] = B[WEIGHT][j];
        --j;
    }
    A[j + 1] = temp;
    B[HEIGHT][j + 1] = tempi[HEIGHT];
    B[WEIGHT][j + 1] = tempi[WEIGHT];
}
```

Solution 3 Pointers. Pointers are another difficult concept to see, but easy to understand once you get over that initial hurdle. There are two ways of implementing pointers. We will only discuss array indices. You keep track of the array index that pointed to each array item.

1. For the above example, you might either have a third column in the HeightWeight Array that holds that rows index to the Name Array. This makes the most sense, since the array index is of type int, and the HeightWeight Array is of type int. Then if the Name array is sorted, the most likely occurrence, this index number is changed to reflect the new position of the relevant name's position in that array. Of course, if you need to sort the HeightWeight Array by Height and then by Weight for instance, you simply maintain the Pointer column and no further action is taken.

```
final static int PTR = 2;
```

Your initial load looks almost the same as the parallel arrays, with the exception of the overhead of adding the additional column. Reading the data resembles the previous examples with the exception of the addition of HeightWeight[NAMEPTR][Size] holds the array index of the Names array.

```
Record = readRecord(Input);
while(Record[1].compareTo("0") > 0) {
        HeightWeight[HEIGHT][Size] =
        convert(Record[1]);
        HeightWeight[WEIGHT][Size] =
        convert(Record[2]);
        HeightWeight[PTR][Size] = Size;
        Names[Size] = Record[0];
        ++Size;
        Record = readRecord(Input);
    } // end While
```

The use code looks very similar, except we need to look up the HeightWeight Position. For that we build a lookup method, You pass in the PTR from Names and it returns the position of the related HeightWeight Record.

```
for(int i = 0; i < size ; ++i){
        if (0 == (A[PTR][i] - ptr)) return i;
}
        return notFound;
}
```

Then the use code looks like:

```
for (int i = 0; i < Size; ++i){
        Name = Names[i];
        position = lookup(Size,i,HeightWeight);
        iHeight = HeightWeight[HEIGHT][position];
        iWeight = HeightWeight[WEIGHT][position];
        BMI = computeBMI(iHeight,iWeight);
        outLine =
String.format(FORMATSTRING,Name,iHeight,iWeight,BMI);
        System.out.println(outLine);
    }
```

Now the insertion sort looks like:

```
for(int i = 1; i < size; i++) {
        j = i - 1;
        temp = A[i];
    p = lookup(size,i,B);
        tempi[HEIGHT] = B[HEIGHT][p];
    tempi[WEIGHT] = B[WEIGHT][p];
    while(j >= 0 &&
    (temp.compareToIgnoreCase(A[j]) < 0)) {
            A[j + 1] = A[j];
            p = lookup(size,j,B);
            pp1 = lookup(size,j+1,B);
                B[HEIGHT][pp1] = B[HEIGHT][p];
                B[WEIGHT][pp1] = B[WEIGHT][p];
            B[PTR][pp1] = j+1;
                --j;
        }
        A[j + 1] = temp;
    pp1 = lookup(size,j+1,B);
    B[HEIGHT][pp1] = tempi[HEIGHT];
    B[WEIGHT][pp1] = tempi[WEIGHT];
    B[PTR][pp1] = j+1;
    }
```

Alternatively, since we normally look at Names first, let us put the pointer in the Names arry. This means that the PTR column will be a String and we will have to convert it when we set it and when we want to use it, but since we would normally want to manipulate the names and then trace data to names, it seems more natural to use our data that way.

We set our PTR constant to 1. And define our two parallel arrays as:

```
String[][] Names = new String[2][FMAXSIZE];
int[][] HeightWeight = new int[2][FMAXSIZE];
```

Our read code now sets our PTR to point from Names to the index of HeightWeight. It does convert the Size variable from int to String.

```
while(Record[1].compareTo("0") > 0) {
        HeightWeight[HEIGHT][Size] =
        convert(Record[1]);
        HeightWeight[WEIGHT][Size] =
        convert(Record[2]);
        Names[NAME][Size] = Record[0];
        Names[HWPTR][Size] = "" + Size;
        ++Size;
        Record = readRecord(Input);
} // end While
```

Our Use method no longer needs the lookup, we do need to convert the Names pointer to int.

```
for (int i = 0; i < Size; ++i){
        Name = Names[NAME][i];
        position = convert(Names[HWPTR][i]);
        iHeight = HeightWeight[HEIGHT][position];
        iWeight = HeightWeight[WEIGHT][position];
        BMI = computeBMI(iHeight,iWeight);
        outLine =
        String.format(FORMATSTRING,Name,iHeight
        ,iWeight,BMI);
        System.out.println(outLine);
}
```

The largest difference that you will see is in the insertion sort. We no longer need to pass the HeightWeight Array along into the sort method. The pointer takes care of that issue.

```
for(int i = 1; i < size; i++) {
j = i - 1;
        temp[NAME] = A[NAME][i];
        temp[HWPTR] = A[HWPTR][i];
        while(j >= 0 &&
(temp[NAME].compareToIgnoreCase(A[NAME][j]) < 0))
{
        A[NAME][j + 1] = A[NAME][j];
        A[HWPTR][j+1] = A[HWPTR][j];
        --j;
 }
 A[NAME][j + 1] = temp[NAME];
 A[HWPTR][j + 1] = temp[HWPTR];
 }
```

2. Another method, (particularly, if none of your arrays were of type int) would be to have an additional array with a column for each array that would hold the index to each of the corresponding arrays. For instance, in our example, you would define:

```
final static int NAMEPTR = 0;
final static int HWPTR = 1;
String[] Names = new String[FMAXSIZE];
int[][] HeightWeight = new int[2][FMAXSIZE];
int[][]  ptrArray = new int[2][FMAXSIZE];
```

Our Read code would look like:

```
Record = readRecord(Input);
while(Record[1].compareTo("0") > 0) {
      HeightWeight[HEIGHT][Size] =
      convert(Record[1]);
      HeightWeight[WEIGHT][Size] =
      convert(Record[2]);
      Names[Size] = Record[0];
      ptrArray[NAMEPTR][Size] = Size;
      ptrArray[HWPTR][Size] = Size;
      ++Size;
      Record = readRecord(Input);
} // end While
```

Obviously we would need a way to lookup the Name, Height, and Weight pointer. I decided that my lookup functions would return the values. So these look up methods resemble:

```
public static int lookupHeight(int input
, int[][] ptrArray, int[][] HeightWeight ){
int position = ptrArray[HWPTR][input];
      return HeightWeight[HEIGHT][position];
}
public static int lookupWeight(int input
, int[][] ptrArray, int[][] HeightWeight ){
int position = ptrArray[HWPTR][input];
      return HeightWeight[WEIGHT][position];
}
public static String lookupName(int input
, int[][] ptrArray, String[] Names ){
      int position = ptrArray[NAMEPTR][input];
      return Names[position];

}
```

Our Use code would look like:

```
for (int i = 0; i < Size; ++i){
        Name = lookupName(i, ptrArray,Names );
        iHeight = lookupHeight(i, ptrArray,
            HeightWeight );
        iWeight = lookupWeight(i, ptrArray,
            HeightWeight );
        BMI = computeBMI(iHeight,iWeight);
        outLine =
String.format(FORMATSTRING,Name,iHeight,iWeight,BMI);
        System.out.println(outLine);
    }
```

The insertion sort is where things get interesting. While, you need the Names array, you only use it for information. You do not move any of the Names entries. You only move the pointers. This may have some nice performance effects, when your array holds large amounts of data, since your arrays hold only integers. This is the reason that RDBMS systems make wide use of indexes. You can also have different pointer arrays with different sort schemes, without affecting the original arrays. So you can end up sorting your data in several different manners simultaneously.

```
for(int i = 1; i < size; i++) {
            j = i - 1;
            temp = lookupName(i, ptrArray,A );
        namePtr = ptrArray[NAMEPTR][i];
        HWPtr = ptrArray[HWPTR][i];
        while(j >= 0 && (temp.compareToIgnoreCase(
lookupName(j, ptrArray,A )) < 0)) {
                ptrArray[NAMEPTR][j + 1] =
ptrArray[NAMEPTR][j];
            ptrArray[HWPTR][j + 1] =
ptrArray[HWPTR][j]
            --j;
            }

            ptrArray[NAMEPTR][j+1] = namePtr;
            ptrArray[HWPTR][j+1] = HWPtr;
    }
```

3. Memory Location Pointers. This is the most natural and understandable way to use pointers. Java does not support this method.

Solution 4. Stamp Data

Stamp Data aka Abstract Data Types aka Java Classes. We introduced this concept in the data types chapter. This Solution allows you to eliminate any overhead and headaches of trying to force data that belongs together by allowing you to build your own data type. In Java this is known as building your own class. There is usually a lot more to it, but for this book, we won't worry about anything other than the data aspects.

Now, like a method, this has to appear in the Class definition, separate from the main. I recommend placing it at the beginning after the class definition after the class brace and before the main definition. Basically where we place the class variables.

```
import CSCI1302.*;
public class myFirstJava
{

// ←==put it here
```

Now the format is like the class definition However, it will have to be declared static, if it was not static, you would have to define it in its own file, itself.

```
public static class classname {

variables

} //end class
```

All of your variables should be public.

136

To use it is just like any non static reference class. First you are going to have to define a variable and instantiate it.

For instance, say we built a class based on our new file

```
public static class NameHeightWeight{
        public String Name;
        public int Height;
        public int Weight;
    } // end class NameHeightWeight
```

To use this class we need to define it in a program and instantiate it.

```
NameHeightWeight record =
    new NameHeightWeight();
```

The class is the template. The instantiated record is termed the object.

We have seen the convention "new classname();" before. This executes a method, the constructor, which can either be defined by java or the programmer, that sets aside memory and initializes all of the variables within the class.

Now to use the data, you use the same object dot variable logic that we have seen before (usually for methods):

```
record.Name = "Kaden Diaz";
record.Height = 65;
record.Weight = 242;
```

And to then use the data:

```
System.out.println(Person.Name + "   " +
Person.Height + "   " + Person.Weight);
```

Now if we needed to build our array to hold all of our people we have a slight problem. Remember arrays can only hold primitive and String values. Our NameHeightWeight class is a reference value. Well, Java has a container class similar to arrays (actually better) called ArrayList that is designed to act like an array but will hold only reference values.

ArrayList

ArrayList has three major benefits over arrays:

1. You do not define a maximum size at compile time. ArrayList grows as you expand it.
2. You can add to or delete from the middle of ArrayList without penalty.
3. Arraylist has a built in method called size() to tell you the current used size of the ArrayList.

The biggest difference in ArrayList is that instead of directly using braces to address the individual members, e.g., [i], you have to use methods, such as:

add(e) adds an element to the next position in the ArrayList.
get(int) gets the element from the position on the Arraylist as specified on the index.
set(int,e) sets the element from the position on the Arraylist as specified on the index.

One hint. When you add a reference type to an Arraylist. Make sure that you create a new element. Otherwise you may end up with an ArrayList with n copies of the same data.

There are other built-in methods, but some of them, such as sorting require you to do additional work on your class type, which is beyond the scope of this course.

The first step in using an ArrayList is to make sure that you import the correct java library.

```
import java.util.*;
```

Defining an ArrayList is a little different than an array. You don't actually set aside space for the ArrayList or define the type of the ArrayList. You do give the compiler a hint of what type to expect using <type>.

```
ArrayList <NameHeightWeight> People =
    new ArrayList<NameHeightWeight>();
```

Note this <Reference Type> is a compiler hint. It is not a runtime instruction. Hence, it is not included in the method signature. Therefore, you cannot have two methods with the same name and the same parameters except for Arraylists with different <Reference Type>;

```
Build(ArrayList<Person>  People);
Build(Arraylist<Dog> Dogs);
```

These two methods are not allowed. Even though Person and Dog are different Reference types.

So the code to read in this file becomes:

```
inputRecord = readRecord(Input);
while(null != inputRecord ) {
    newRecord = new record();
    newRecord.Name = inputRecord[0];
    newRecord.Height =
    convert(inputRecord[1]);
    newRecord.Weight =
    convert(inputRecord[2]);
    People.add(newRecord);
    inputRecord = readRecord(Input);
} // end While
```

The code to use the data:

```
for (int i = 0; i < Size; ++i){
    myRecord = People.get(i);
    Name = myRecord.Name;
    iHeight = myRecord.Height;
    iWeight = myRecord.Weight;
```

```
            BMI = computeBMI(iHeight,iWeight);
            outLine =
String.format(FORMATSTRING,Name,iHeight,iWeight,BMI);
            System.out.println(outLine);
    }
```

And this really simplifies the insertion sort:

```
    for(int i = 1; i < Size; i++) {
        j = i - 1;
        temp = People.get(i);
    while(j >= 0 &&
    (temp.Name.compareToIgnoreCase
    (lookupName(j, People)) < 0)) {
        myRecord = People.get(j);
        People.set(j+1,myRecord);
        --j;
    }
    People.set(j+1,temp);
    }
```

The lookup method is just used to clean up the compare. It holds the get:

```
    public static String lookupName(int input,
        ArrayList <record> People){
        record myRecord;
        myRecord = People.get(input);
        return myRecord.Name;

    }
```

Personally, I really like this last solution. Especially where it relates data to file structures. You will note:

1. The file structure is clearly denoted by the class. It is not hidden.
2. It is always clear what the variables are.
3. It is always clear that the heights and weights are related to a single individual without any additional coding.
4. If the file structure changes, then you simply need to change the class and the input method.

There is a lot more to classes and objects. There is a lot more to Java. But this is only one course. It is time to turn our attention to how to take what we have learned to solve problems and look at methodologies.

Review

We have gone from one dimension arrays to multidimensional arrays. We saw that it wasn't much of a stretch. They are still limited to the following characteristics:

1. Using one data type per array.
2. Using either primitive data types or strings
3. Unable to add or remove data from the middle.
4. Must set the maximum size of the array at compile time.
5. Must keep track of the actual size of the array manually.

While your outermost row can be ragged, you should remember that the size of your array grows multiplicatively. When you define a 10 x 10 x 10 array, you end up with 1,000 elements. If it is of type double, 64 bits or 8 bytes each, that is about 8K for the Array. If you multiply each dimension by 10, 100 x 100 x 100, you end up with 8G. So you see that these can grow very fast.

Rarely are you only dealing with one data type, you may encounter, configuration data, statistics, bills of sale, etc. We discussed four ways of handling this issue.

1. Convert all data to String.
2. Use multiple synchronized arrays.
3. Use multiple arrays with integer pointers.
4. Use multiple arrays with actual pointers.
5. Use stamp data aka java classes.

I personally feel that stamp data or the java class gives you the cleanest method for handling the data most of the time. Note: No one solution is the right answer all of the time.

Since java classes are reference data, we had to introduce ArrayLists as a companion to arrays. ArrayLists allow you to:

1. Hold reference types (not primitive types)
2. Add or remove data from the middle of the ArrayList.
3. Avoid setting the maximum size of the ArrayList..
4. Provides a built in function, size(), for the actual size of the ArrayList.

Questions

1. When you look at two-dimensional arrays you can visualize them using:
    a. A book.
    b. An Excel spreadsheet
    c. A Filing cabinet
    d. A Desk
2. When using a two-dimensional array it is legal to:
    a. Have one column string and one integer
    b. Have one column string and one column string holding an integer
    c. Both a and b
    d. None of the above.
3. When using pointers.
    a. You need one column to have an integer in every array to hold the array index to the other array.
    b. You need one column to have an integer in at least one array to hold the array index to every other array.
    c. You must always have an additional array to have the array index for every other array.
    d. None of the above
4. A non-integer pointer holds:
    a. The actual memory address of the data that it points to.
    b. The position of the integer index.
    c. The data.
5. Arraylists belong to
    a. java.array.*;
    b. java.util.*;
    c. java.lang.*;
    d. java.collections.*;
6. If Name is a variable in object Person, how do you access it?
    a. Person.Name()
    b. Person.Name
    c. Name
    d. Name.Person

7. If you have a two dimensional Array of String[2][] Person where the Person[0][] is Name and Person[1][] is Height, how could I get the height from Person[i] as an integer?
   a.   (int) Person[1][i]
   b.   Person[i].Height
   c.   CSCIConvert.Parse(Person[1][i],0)
   d.   a and c.
   e.   None of the above
8. If I have two Synchronized Arrays Person[] and Height[] and I need the Height for Person[i] how do I get it.
   a.   Height[i]
   b.   Height[Person[i].index]
   c.   CSCIConvert.Parse(Height[i],0)
   d.   None of the above
9. Suppose I have an index Index[2][] which is used to synchronize Person and Height. If I have Person[i] how would I get its related Height. Index[0][i] points to Person. Index[1][i] points to Height.
   a.   Search Index[0][] until I found i at Index[0][j] then Height[Index[1][j]]
   b.   Height[[index[0][i]]
   c.   Height[index[1][i]]
   d.   None of the above
10. If you have a class Person completely instantiate an object Boy
   a.   Boy Person;
   b.   Person Boy;
   c.   Person Boy = new Person();
   d.   Boy Person = new Boy();

Problems

Compile, debug, and run these problems

1. Build a program that uses a two dimensional array to hold the height and width of ten rectangles and display the Areas of each rectangle. The program should read pairs ten integers values from a file. The file should have ten pairs of integers separated by a comma like:

```
34,2
41,56
55,25
37,62
10,64
34,89
68,63
56,8
71,56
17,55
```

2. Build a program that reads in the data in nameageweight.csv and finds the top ten heaviest people and prints out their names, ages and weights. Hint. You may want to break out the weights into a separate array and use Arrays.sort(). The data in this file looks like:

```
Kelly,40,155
Karen,5,191
Quemby,76,150
Hedda,38,124
Marah,79,167
Victoria,30,147
Quintessa,87,200
Wang,82,139
```

Chapter 10. Software Engineering

Projects

Every project is going to have a number of factors to consider, but the big three are always"

Time
Budget
Quality

It is usually difficult to find a balance between these three critical factors and bring in a quality product on time and under budget. What does a quality product mean?

Quality Product

1. It must meet the requirements. What are the requirements?
    Like a school assignment, the requirements are those detailed

items that dictate what the software must accomplish and in what way it must accomplish those items. We will get into more detail shortly.

2. It must contain minimal errors after the project is implemented. Errors or bugs as they are commonly known are anything that goes wrong with the program. If you have spent any time working with a computer, you have probably encountered a few, such as, your computer freezing up, or restarting suddenly are extreme examples of errors. Errors generally come in three areas:
    a. Programming or coding errors.
    b. Logic errors.
    c. Requirement errors

3. It must be maintainable. You or someone else must be able to pick up your code and read and understand it six months or a year after you write it. They must be able to fix issues or modify it to meet new requirements.

Software Development Process

Before we begin, I need to let you in on a big secret. Coding is actually a small part of the software development timeline. In my experience, we used to schedule no more than 25% of the time for coding.

Developing software is a never-ending quest for perfection. Ever since computer software started, people have been trying to improve the software development process. In my experience, I have probably been exposed to five or six different methodologies. In my opinion, at their heart, they all are varieties of the waterfall process, so this is what I will expose you to with one slight variance.

The waterfall process recognizes that like building a skyscraper it is more expensive to fix problems or make changes the more of the building is built. For instance, it is significantly more expensive to move bathrooms from one side to the other after the skyscraper is finished than while you are developing the blueprints.

There is an additional psychological factor in that people spend more effort working when a deadline is looming. So instead of only having one deadline, the finish date, it is helpful to add reviews to make sure that measurable amounts of work are completed along the way.

There are some major issues with the waterfall method that other methodologies have attempted to fix:

1. Customers find it hard to visualize and sign off on requirements early.
2. Customers and management fail to understand that any changes to requirements will cost time and money.
3. Customers and management perceive that for a long period of time nothing useful, e.g., software, is produced.
4. Everyone wants to get to the solution early.

Waterfall Process

The Waterfall Process consists of five phases:

1. Analysis
2. Design
3. Code
4. Test
5. Implementation

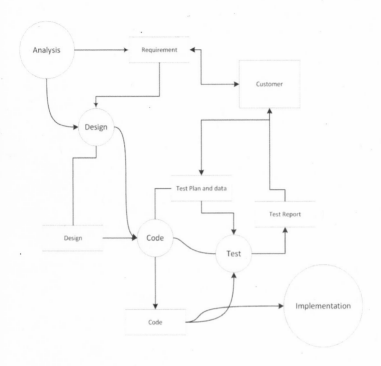

Analysis means collecting and understanding requirements. Requirements are everything that the software needs to accomplish. They include everything from:

1. Inputs
2. Outputs: Reports, Files
3. Databases
4. GUIs
5. Business Logic
6. System Requirements
7. Performance Requirements
8. User lists
9. Security Requirements

You usually end this phase with an analysis review to get changes and a sign off on the requirements document from the customer. This should be treated as a contract between you and the customer.

I quite often combine some of the preliminary design with analysis to accomplish three things:

1. Give the customer ideas for requirement definition.
2. Check requirement viability.
3. Quantify requirements.

You also sometimes build mock-ups of the GUI designs during this phase to get customer input on requirement and design options. Beware, some customers believe that the mock-ups are not throw-away code and believe that you are closer to the final product than you really are. Don't make these dog and pony shows look too good.

Design means determining the best way to accomplish all of the requirements. Usually you start by breaking up the requirements into manageable sets of functionality and then designing each one separately. You might have a separate design team for each function. You then have to have an interface defined so that the functionality will be able to talk to each other. The things you need to worry about are:

1. Addressing as many design ideas as you can, so that you don't miss a good idea.
2. Selecting a design idea that maps back to all of your requirements.
3. Identifying any missing requirements. (You either have to address them in your design, get sign off on missing requirements or design new functionality.)
4. Completing the design idea to the level that it can be coded.
5. Testing the design idea to ensure that it meets the requirements.

Some of the outputs from design are:

1. High level design documentation
2. Low level design Documentation (code Ready).
3. Test cases – mapped to requirements. All testable requirements should be tested.
4. Draft test plan

You probably have two design reviews during the design phase, a high level design review and a final design review.

Code means writing the code to the design. Making certain that it is written to the design standards. Make sure that is well documented and that it compiles and runs.

You usually have a code review with either your peers and or your quality assurance (QA) section as you complete your code.

Output from this phase is usually completed code and test plans and test data.

My variation of the process combines code, unit testing, and integration testing into the same phase. Systems testing and user testing are kept as a separate phase. This is because I believe in performing code and test as I write each method as a much more effective coding methodology than just coding a large block. This has the following advantages:

1. It is much easier to detect, debug and fix code in smaller chunks of code.
2. It is easier (and faster) to fix issues in the last 10% of your code if you are confident that the first 90% is working.
3. Even in a single module, if you code to a point, compile and test it, fix any problems, then add more code, it is faster than writing the whole thing and then trying to fix all of the problems.
4. You can validate your test data early by seeing problems at a much lower level. Which is better than trying to run tests later.

There are two tools used to build/test code:

1. Stubs. Stubs are methods that use the same name, calling parameters, and return type as your designed method, but have no body. Usually, they consist of something to tell you what parameters are sent into them and return a reasonable return type. Sometimes, you can get fancy and have an internal flag variable (usually a temporary global variable) that changes the return variable to an error value. For example:

```
public static int myMethod(String ChangeMe){

System.out.println(
" inside MyMethod - ChangeMe = " + ChangeMe );
return 0;
}//myMethod
```

2. Test Program. A test Program is just a small test Program that calls your method with various inputs to check it out. I usually use this method of testing when I am trying out a new coding concept and not sure how it works.

Test. This means testing against requirements. You or the test group follow the test plan written earlier and report any bugs which are then repaired and retested until a certain quality point (or an arbitrary date) is reached. A quality point is usually defined as a maximum percentage of bugs reported in a period of time. The output of this phase is the completed test report. It is usually broken out into four types of testing:

1. Unit Testing. Testing each piece of code independently.
2. Integration Testing. Joining pieces of code together and testing them together. This is usually joining individual programs together.
3. Systems Testing. Testing the entire system as a whole. This usually includes hardware, software, and possibly different groups prior to user testing.

4. Performance testing. Testing normal and expected workload against any performance requirements. Examples include response time, batch processing time, wait times on database queries or page loads, etc.
5. Stress Testing – Testing your system to find out when or if it will break. Increasing the number of users, or the amount of data that you input until the system breaks or until the number is so high that you would "never" exceed that limit. This is the one time that you are not really unhappy to break your system as long as it doesn't break too early.
6. Load Testing. This is related to performance and stress testing, except that it normally happens in a shared environment. You are usually start the test system with a normal background load of other processes and then ramp up your users to test performance degradation. You usually also look at low and peak system usage trends. These usage estimates are determined by monitoring the live system, before you add your new or modified system.
7. User Testing. This is testing the user interfaces with a small set of actual users from each business unit.
8. Acceptance Testing. This set of tests proves to your user that your system meets his requirements. It is usually monitored by him or his representatives.

Implementation. The completed code, related data, and hardware is sent to and made operational in the field. This can be a simple or extremely complex task.

This methodology can be a complex process. However, depending on the project you can follow the process and still produce quality code in a timely manner.

Conclusion. In my experience, after you gain experience with a process, you can build quality software faster, with fewer errors than not following a process, thus meeting your requirements. And that is the goal.

Review

Meeting your customer's requirements is the actual goal of computer science. Without customers, we wouldn't have computers to play with, or any real reason to write code. You, yourselves, are customers and have almost certainly suffered at the hands of poorly developed software.

I became an early advocate for quality software development. I saw the effects of not having a good process, and was taught several excellent processes. I have seen how a good process creates quality software, on time, and under budget. I have seen it, in the right hands, be flexible, and produce quality code that meets the customer's requirements in record time. On the other hand, I have also seen projects flounder and fail without a good process. Every project has three often-competing factors:

> Quality
> Time
> Budget

We attempt to meet them using a methodology. One of the oldest, that we learned about is the Waterfall, which has five phases:

1. Analysis
2. Design
3. Code
4. Test
5. Implementation

We learned that

1. Analysis was all about gathering and understanding requirements
2. Design was building a design to satisfy requirements.
3. Code is building code to the design and building the inputs for the test phase
4. Test is both ensuring that your code is error free and that it meets the requirements.
5. Implementation is making it available to your customers.

By combing code and unit and integration test together in a process that I call write a little/test a little, we learned that we can reduce code errors significantly and make coding faster.

Test has several flavors including:

1. Unit Testing.
2. Integration Testing.
3. Systems Testing.
4. Performance testing.
5. Load Testing.
6. Stress Testing.
7. User Testing.
8. Acceptance Testing.

Final thoughts.

Now you may see why I said that coding is only about 25% of a projects budget. It is significant, but it is not where most of the skull sweat comes in. Don't get me wrong, I love to program. I love to see my ideas come to life, but my personal favorite part of software development is design.

I have actually seen a multi-million-dollar project scrapped because a high-level customer did not like a GUI design during acceptance testing. Was he involved in the requirements or design? I do not know, but that was the reason given. This is why I like to modularize my design and make the user interfaces completely separate from the business logic.

I also like to mock up the GUI and report look and feel during requirements analysis and get them signed off on as soon as possible. I may need to get changes approved later, but this is the part of the system that your customer has the most interest in.

Questions

1. Analysis is the phase in which:
   a. You design your process.
   b. You develop your code.
   c. You define your requirements.
   d. You test your code to ensure that it meets the requirements.
2. Cohesion means:
   a. How modules communicate between each other.
   b. How many things a module can do.
   c. How modules are compiled.
   d. How you set your comments.
3. Design is the phase in which:
   a. You design your process.
   b. You develop your code.
   c. You define your requirements.
   d. You test your code to ensure that it meets the requirements.
4. When writing code, it is more efficient to:
   a. Write it all, then compile and test and debug it.
   b. Write, compile, test, and debug as you go.
   c. Write the code, then send it to a friend to debug.
   d. Give up and get a new job.
5. Test is the phase in which:
   a. You design your process.
   b. You develop your code.
   c. You define your requirements.
   d. You test your code to ensure that it meets the requirements.
6. The three factors that all projects have in common are:
   a. Quality, time, and budget.
   b. Management, code, and schedule.
   c. Quality, time, and code.
   d. Quality, schedule, and time
   e. Time, budget, and code.

7. Code is the phase in which:
   a. You design your process.
   b. You develop your code.
   c. You define your requirements.
   d. You test your code to ensure that it meets the requirements.
8. In design, when looking at ideas:
   a. Always hone in on the first idea that you come up with.
   b. Always take the senior person's idea.
   c. Look for as many ideas as you can and evaluate them equally.
   d. Skip this step and code.
9. When designing test cases, which statement is false:
   a. Avoid test cases that might make your code fail.
   b. Look for outlier test cases.
   c. Use live test data.
   d. Use extreme amounts of test data.
10. When you are building your design, you should:
   a. Hide it from your customer.
   b. Show as much of it as you can to your customer.
   c. Show it to your buddies from the competition.
   d. Show it to the guy down at the corner.

Appendix A. Using the CCGA Flashdrive.

For the CCGA CSCI classes, we created a Flashdrive with
Notepad++, the Java Developer Kit, the CSCI package and some
example programs get started. You should be able to use this
Flashdrive on your home computer or on any Windows Computer.

Notepad++

NotePad++ is a context driven Text editor that will help you write your Java
source code. While you can use any text editor to write source code, you
cannot use Word to do this.

To bring up Notepad++ bring up the Flashdrive in a FileExplorer Window
and click on the notepad++.exe -Shortcut. Alternatively, go to the
NotepadPP subdirectory, and click on notepad++.exe. You can also left
copy this and then paste a shortcut in the main flashdrive directory.
Notepad++ is fairly easy to use. For further explanation, go to
https://notepad-plus-plus.org/.

data	6/21/2016 14:19	File folder		
java	11/23/2015 14:35	File folder		
NotepadPP	5/24/2016 09:29	File folder		
user	5/24/2016 09:42	File folder		
javasetup.bat	8/16/2016 15:45	Windows Batch File	1 KB	
javasetup.txt	5/24/2016 09:41	Text Document	1 KB	
notepad++.exe - Shortcut	8/16/2016 15:44	Shortcut	1 KB	

Always open your files from the open command in NotePad++. Most of the
school computers do not recognize the .java extension.

You can set your default directory to be user in settings.

Using the Java compiler

To use the Java compiler go to the search window in Windows and type in "cmd", which will bring up the command window.

Note the drive that Windows assigned your flash drive,

Assume F is the drive that Windows assigned to your flash drive. Assume that > is the cursor.

In the Command Window type

```
F:   (or whatever drive the flash is on)
cd user
```

type

```
cd user
```

now open javasetup.txt and copy and paste the contents into your command window.

javasetup.txt consists of two lines:

```
set CLASSPATH=./;
set PATH=Path;..\java\bin\;..\Notepadd\Notepad++
```

Note: CLASSPATH is a variable that tells the Java compiler where to look for any packages, such as CSCI. If you are working in user CSCI is in user/CSCI. If you are not in user you must move CSCI to be a subdirectory under your directory or change the subdirectory.

Likewise, if you move the level of directory that you are working on, you will have to change the path.

For this reason, it is much simpler if you plan on working in user.

The java compiler is javac. myFirstJava is an empty, commented, program class (an empty program is termed a shell). It sits in the file, myFirstJava.java, in the user directory. To compile this program, you type:

> `javac myFirstJava.java`

Then you debug any errors. Once it is debugged, you run it using the java interpreter

> `java myFirstJava`

Now notice, that nothing will happen with this shell. However, a shell is a handy thing to have since it can be used to ensure that you have the right format. If you use the shell, I would change the class name and save it with the new class name to preserve the shell for future use.

What is on the flash drive?

CSCI package see Appendix C
Hello.java
myFirstJava.java

Hello.java
```
public class Hello
{

    public static void main(String[] args)
    {
      System.out.println("Hello");
    }
}
```

myFirstJava.java

```
import CSCI.*;
public class myFirstJava
{
//  This program shell is to allow you to write a
Java program.
//  Change the class name.  And save it as the new
name.java  don't forget capitalization.

    public static void main(String[] args ) {
    //  Variable definitions

    //  code

} //end main

// any methods go here

} //end myFirstJava
```

Appendix B Java Reserved Words

abstract

assert

boolean

break

byte

case

catch

char

class

const

continue

default

do

double

else

enum

extends

final

finally

float

for

goto

if

implements

import

instanceof

int

interface

long

native

new

package

private

protected

public

return

short

static

strictfp

super

switch

synchronized

this

throw

throws

transient

try

void

volatile

while

Appendix C CSCI Package.

The CSCI Package is a set of Utilities built to simplify coding in the CCGA courses. These utilities were designed to allow the students to code functionality before certain topics were presented and simplify their code.

To use the package:

1. Have the directory CSCI with all .java and/or .class files in your compilation directory.
2. You can compile the .java files by typing:

> `java CSCI\*.java`

3. include the statement

    import CSCI.*;

before the class definition.

CSCI currently includes the following classes

(Note: these are static utility classes and do not need to be instantiated to be used.)

    AgeUtility
        Date getBirthDate(String);
        Integer getAge(Date);
        String getAgeString(Date);
        String getBirthDateString(Date);
    CSCIConvert
        boolean IsNotInt(String);
        boolean IsNotDouble(String);
        int Parse(String, int);
        double Parse(String, double);

CSCIMath
    double GetAverage(int, int[]);
    double GetAverage(ArrayList<Integer>);
    double GetAverage(int, double[]);
    double GetMedian(ArrayList<Integer>);
    double GetMedian(int, int[]);
    double GetMedian(int, double[]);
    int GetMax(int, int[]);
    double GetMax(int, double[]);
    int GetMax(ArrayList<Integer>);
    int GetMin(int, int[]);
    double GetMin(int, double[]);
    int GetMin(ArrayList<Integer>);
DisplayTime
    String now()
    Long nowMS()

The last several are non-static classes and need to be instantiated to be used.

keyBoard reads data from the keyboard. It has various safe methods to read a single line of input of data.

keyBoard
    keyBoard();
    String read();
    String readUpperCase();
    String readLowerCase();
    char read(char);
    char readLowerCase(char);
    char readUpperCase(char);
    int read(int);
    double read(double);
    boolean read(boolean);

Menu's Constructors accept either an array size, and a menu option array and menu option description array, or single option and description.

    Menu
        Menu(int, String[], String[]);
        Menu(String, String);
        project();

TitleMenu's Constructors are the same as Menu except that the first variable, is the menu title.

    TitleMenu extends Menu
        TitleMenu(String, int, String[], String[]);
        TitleMenu(String, String, String);
        project();

These constructors will accept either a (FileName) or (Directory, Filename) to set them up:

    FileIn
        FileIn(String);
        FileIn(String, String);
        String Read();
        void close();
    FileOut
        FileOut(String);
        FileOut(String, String);
        void Write(String);
        void close();

Appendix D Resources

I made extensive use of the Oracle Documentation site to verify my concepts and Ideas.

http://docs.oracle.com/javase/7/docs/api/

I learned Java from

Learning Java by Niemeyer and Leueck

I firmly believe that one of the finest books on Software engineering is

The Mythical Man Month by Frederick P. Brooks Jr.

I have used the following books in my classes over the past few years and concepts have affected this book:

Problem Solving and Programming Concepts by Mareen Sprangle and Jim Hubbard

Java Programming by Joyce Farrell

Over the past thirty some odd years, I have read more books and taken more courses than I can count or remember. All of these courses and books have influenced this book to some degree or another.

Oracle Java JDK Download Site

http://www.oracle.com/technetwork/java/javase/downloads/index.html

Use this site to download the latest Java JDK. The JDK is the Development Kit. It has the necessary executables and support files for the java compiler and the virtual machine.

Warning: After you have run the JDK, you still may need to make sure that javac is part of your path in order to use it. Example: You may need to add C:\Program Files\Java\jdk1.8.0_65\bin to the Path Variable in your Environment Variables.

NotePad++ official Site

https://notepad-plus-plus.org/

This is the official site for the Notepad++ download and is a free download.

Appendix E Radio Alphabet

A,Alpha
B,Bravo
C,Charlie
D,Delta
E,Echo
F,Foxtrot
G,Golf
H,Hotel
I,India
J,Juliet
K,Kilo
L,Lima
M,Mike
N,November
O,Oscar
P,Papa
Q,Quebec
R,Romeo
S,Sierra
T,Tango
U,Uniform
V,Victor
W,Whiskey
X,X-ray
Y,Yankee
Z,Zulu

Appendix F Vocabulary

Term	Definition
Algorithm	A solution to a problem that can be solved through a sequence of instructions.
Algorithmic solution	A sequence of instructions to solve a problem. A computer programmer writes a solution in the form of an algorithm before coding it into a computer language.
Array	Sometimes called a subscripted variable; a block of memory locations in the internal memory that is assigned to one variable name. Arrays may be one-dimensional, twodimensional, or multidimensional.
Assembly language	A three-letter representation of a machine language instruction.
Base-one system	A computer system in which array element numbers begin with one rather than zero.
Base-zero system	A computer system in which element numbers begin with zero rather than one.
Batch processing	Running successive sets of data through a program all at one time without human intervention.
Binary search	A technique used to search for a single element in an array or a single record in a file.
Bug	An error in a computer program.
Calculation module	A Process module that does arithmetic calculations and accumulates, counts, or manipulates numeric data in some way.
Case logic structure	One of the four logic structures for organizing the instructions to the computer that make up a program. The case structure allows the computer to select one set of instructions from among many, through data given by the user or calculated in the solution.
cast operator	an operator that performs an explicit type conversion; it is created by placing the desired result type in parentheses before the expression to be converted.

char	the data type that holds any single character.
character	any letter, number, or special symbol (such as a punctuation mark) that comprises data.
Character data	The data set of the character data type; it includes all symbols available on a computer.
Class	A class is part of a solution of an object-oriented solution to a problem. A class models the properties or characteristics of a set of objects.
class body	the set of data items and methods between the curly braces that follow the class header.
class definition	a description of attributes and methods of objects instantiated from a class. the top section contains the name of the class, the middle section contains the names and data types of the attributes, and the bottom section contains the methods.
Class diagram	A UML diagram that describes the structure of a system with its classes, attributes, and class relationships.
class methods	static methods that do not have a this reference (because they have no object associated with them).
class user	an application or class that instantiates objects of another prewritten class. See also class client.
class variables	static variables that are shared by every instantiation of a class.
close the file	to make a file no longer available to an application.
Cohesion	Concept that a method has one purpose and its independence from other methods.
collision	describes a class naming conflict.
Concatenation	Adding one piece of string data to another by placing the second piece immediately after the first.
Constant	A value in a program that cannot change during processing.
Control module	The module controlling the processing of all of the subtasks in a solution.
counting	the process of continually incrementing a variable to keep track of the number of occurrences of some event.

Coupling	Concept of how any two modules communicate with each other.
crash	a premature, unexpected, and inelegant end to a program.
Data	Unorganized facts.
data fields	data variables declared in a class outside of any method.
data files	files that consist of related records that contain facts and figures, such as employee numbers, names, and salaries.
data type	describes the type of data that can be stored in a variable, how much memory the item occupies, and what types of operations can be performed on the data.
Data type	The kind of data of a variable or a constant. The three basic data types are numeric, character, and logical.
Data Validation module	Module that Checks data to make sure it is correct
Database Management System (DBMS)	Software that stores large quantities of data, organizes data, and prints reports.
dead code	unreachable statements.
Debugging	The process of correcting errors in a computer program.
decimal numbering system	the numbering system based on 10 digits, 0 through 9, in which each column value is 10 times the value of the column to its right.
Decision logic structure	One of the four logic structures for organizing the instructions to the computer that make up a program. The decision structure selects one of two sets of instructions according to the resultant of a condition.
Decision table	A programming aid to writing decision instructions for the computer; it consists of a rectangular grid divided into four parts, which specifies all possible actions the computer could take for each possible set of conditions.

declaration	another name for a method header; also, the statement that assigns a data type and identifier to a variable.
decrementing	the act of subtracting 1 from a variable.
default constructor	a constructor that requires no arguments.
default package	the unnamed package in which a class is placed if no package is specified.
Default value	A value of a variable that is built into a program and that the computer automatically uses unless the value is changed by the user.
definite loop	a loop that executes a predetermined number of times; a counted loop. Contrast with indefinite loop.
descending order	the order of objects arranged from highest to lowest value. See also ascending order.
development environment	a set of tools that helps programmers by providing such features as displaying a language's keywords in color.
directories	elements in a storage organization hierarchy. See also folders.
do...while loop	a loop that executes a loop body at least one time; it checks the loop control variable at the bottom of the loop after one repetition has occurred.
documentation comments	comments that automatically generate well-formatted program documentation.
do-nothing loop	a loop that performs no actions other than looping.
double	a data type that can hold a floating-point value of up to 14 or 15 significant digits of accuracy. Contrast with float.
double-precision floating-point number	a type of value that is stored in a double.
dummy values	values the user enters that are not "real" data, but just signals to stop data entry.
Dynamic array	An array in which the maximum number of elements can change during processing.

dynamic method binding	the ability of an application to select the correct subclass method when the program executes. See also late method binding.
dynamically resizable	describes an object whose size can change during program execution.
echoing the input	the act of repeating the user's entry as output so the user can visually confirm the entry's accuracy.
element	one variable or object in an array.
else clause	the part of an if...else statement that executes when the evaluated Boolean expression is false.
else...if clause	a format used in nested if statements in which each instance of else and its subsequent if are placed on the same line.
empty body	a block with no statements in it.
empty statement	a statement that contains only a semicolon.
encapsulation	the act of hiding data and methods within an object.
EndOfFile (EOF)	The marker in a computer solution indicating that there are no more records to be processed.
Equation	A variable that is assigned the value of an expression, another variable, or a constant, as in A = 5 + B, A = B (where B is a variable), or A = 5, respectively.
equivalency operator	the operator composed of two equal signs that compares values and returns true if they are equal.
escape sequence	a sequence that begins with a backslash followed by a character; the pair frequently represents a nonprinting character.
event-driven program	a program in which the user might initiate any number of events in any order.
exception	in object-oriented terminology, an unexpected or error condition.
exception handling	an object-oriented technique for managing or resolving errors.

exception specification	the practice of using the keyword throws followed by an Exception type in the method header. An exception specification is required when a method throws a checked Exception that it will not catch but will be caught by a different method.
executing	the act of carrying out a program statement or program.
explicit conversion	the data type transformation caused by using a cast operator.
Expression	An operation or series of operations performed on variables or constants, as in 5 + B.
extended	describes classes that have descended from another class.
extends	a keyword used to achieve inheritance in Java.
External documentation	Instructions to the user in the form of manuals or other written documents.
FAQs	frequently asked questions.
fault-tolerant	describes applications that are designed so that they continue to operate, possibly at a reduced level, when some part of the system fails.
field	a data variable declared in a class outside of any method. In reference to storage, a group of characters that has some meaning.
File	A collection of related records.
final	the keyword that precedes named constants, that describes superclass methods that cannot be overridden in a subclass, and describes classes in which all methods are final.
finally block	a block of code that executes at the end of a try...catch sequence.
fixed method binding	the opposite of dynamic method binding; it occurs when a subclass method is selected while the program compiles rather than while it is running. See also static method binding.
flag	a variable that holds a value (often true or false) to indicate whether some condition has been met.

float	a data type that can hold a floating- point value of up to six or seven significant digits of accuracy. Contrast with double.
floating-point	describes a number that contains decimal positions.
floating-point division	the operation in which two values are divided and either or both are floating-point values.
flowchart	a tool that helps programmers plan a program's logic by writing the steps in diagram form, as a series of shapes connected by arrows.
flushing	an operation to clear bytes that have been sent to a buffer for output but that have not yet been output to a hardware device.
folders	elements in a storage organization hierarchy. See also directories.
for loop	a loop that can be used when a definite number of loop iterations is required.
foreach loop	the enhanced for loop.
formal parameters	the variables in a method declaration that accept the values from actual parameters. Contrast with actual parameters.
format string	in a printf() statement, a string of characters that includes optional text (that is displayed literally) and one or more format specifiers.
fragile	describes classes that are prone to errors.
fully qualified identifier	describes a filename that includes the entire hierarchy in which a class is stored.
fundamental classes	basic classes contained in the java.lang package that are automatically imported into every program. Contrast with optional classes.
garbage value	the unknown value stored in an uninitialized variable.
generic programming	a feature of languages that allows methods to be used safely with multiple data types.
Global variable	A variable that can be accessed by all modules below and in line (in the interactivity chart) with the module that declared the variable.

goes out of scope	describes what happens to a variable at the end of the block in which it is declared. Contrast with comes into scope.
graphical user interfaces (GUIs)	environments that allow users to interact with a program in a graphical environment.
GUI components	graphical user interface components, such as buttons and text fields, with which the user can interact.
hardware	the general term for computer equipment.
has-a relationship	a relationship based on composition.
hash code	a calculated number used to identify an object.
Hashing	A method of using a predefined algorithm to designate the record number for fast retrieval of a given record.
header	the first line of a method; its declaration.
Heuristic solution	A solution to a problem that cannot be solved through a single sequence of instructions.
hexadecimal numbering system	a numbering system based on 16 digits, 0 through F, in which each column represents a value 16 times higher than the column to its right.
Hierarchy	The order in which operations are performed for mathematical, relational, and logical operations.
high-level programming language	a language that uses a vocabulary of reasonable terms, such as read, write, or add, instead of referencing the sequences of on and off switches that perform these tasks. Contrast with low-level programming language.
HTML (Hypertext Markup Language)	a simple language used to create Web pages.
identifier	the name of a program component such as a class, object, or variable.
if clause	the part of an if. . .else statement that executes when the evaluated Boolean expression is true.

if...else statement	a statement that provides the mechanism to perform one action when a Boolean expression evaluates as true, and to perform a different action when a Boolean expression evaluates as false.
immutable	describes objects that cannot be changed.
implementation	the actions that execute within a method; the method body.
implementation hiding	a principle of object-oriented programming that describes the encapsulation of method details within a class.
implicit conversion	the automatic transformation of one data type to another. Also called promotion.
import statement	a Java statement that allows access to a built-in Java class that is contained in a package.
inclusion polymorphism	the situation in which a single method implementation can be used with a variety of related objects because they are objects of subclasses of the parameter type. See also pure polymorphism.
Incrementing	The process of counting on the computer by adding a number to a previous number. The instruction for incrementing by one is Counter = Counter + 1.
indefinite loop	a loop in which the final number of iterations is unknown. Contrast with definite loop.
index	a subscript.
Indicator	A value built into a solution by the programmer to redirect the flow of processing.
infinite loop	a loop that never ends.
Information	Organized facts.
information hiding	the object-oriented programming principle used when creating private access for data fields; a class's private data can be changed or manipulated only by a class's own methods, and not by methods that belong to other classes.
inheritance	a mechanism that enables one class to inherit, or assume, both the behavior and the attributes of another class.

initialization	the act of making an assignment at the time of variable declaration.
initialization list	a series of values provided for an array when it is declared.
Initialization module	The module containing all of the processing that has to be completed only once and at the beginning of the solution.
inner block	a block contained in an outer block.
inner classes	nested classes that require an instance. See also nonstatic member classes.
inner loop	a loop that is contained entirely within another loop.
insertion sort	a sorting algorithm that operates by comparing each list element with earlier ones and, if the element is out of order, opening a spot for it by moving all subsequent elements down the list.
instance	an existing object of a class.
instance methods	methods used with object instantiations. See also nonstatic methods.
instance variables	the data components of a class.
instantiation	the process of creating an object.
int	the data type used to declare variables and constants that store integers in the range of −2,147,483,648 to +2,147,483,647.
integer	a whole number without decimal places.
integer division	the operation in which one integer value is divided by another; the result contains no fractional part.
Interactive processing	Processing that involves user intervention to enter new data as needed, usually at a keyboard.
interactive program	a program in which the user makes direct requests.
Interactivity chart	A chart, also called a structure chart, showing all of the subtasks, or modules, in a program.

interface	a construct similar to a class, except that all of its methods must be abstract and all of its data (if any) must be static final; it declares method headers, but not the instructions within those methods. Also used to describe the part of a method that a client sees and uses. it includes the method's return type, name, and arguments.
Internal documentation	Remarks within a computer solution to explain the processing.
interpreter	a program that translates language statements into machine code. An interpreter translates and executes one statement at a time. Contrast with compiler.
invoke	to call or execute a method.
is-a relationship	the relationship between an object and the class of which it is a member.
iteration	one loop execution. J
Java	an object-oriented programming language used both for general-purpose business applications and for interactive, World Wide Web-based Internet applications.
Java API	the application programming interface, a collection of information about how to use every prewritten Java class.
Java applications	stand-alone Java programs.
Java ARchive (JAR) file	a file that compresses the stored data.
Java interpreter	the program that checks bytecode and communicates with the operating system, executing the bytecode instructions line by line within the Java Virtual Machine.
Java Virtual Machine (JVM)	a hypothetical (software-based) computer on which Java runs.
java.lang	the package that is implicitly imported into every Java program and that contains the fundamental classes.

Javadoc	a documentation generator that creates Application Programming Interface (API) documentation in Hypertext Markup Language (HTML) format from Java source code.
Javadoc comment	a special form of block comment that provides a standard way to document Java code.
Javadoc tag	a keyword within a comment that the Javadoc tool can process.
JDK	the Java Standard Edition Development Kit.
Key	The field of the records that is used to order a file or search for a record.
key field	the field in a record that makes the record unique from all others.
keyboard buffer	a small area of memory where keystrokes are stored before they are retrieved into a program. Also called the type-ahead buffer.
keywords	the words that are part of a programming language.
late method binding	the ability of an application to select the correct subclass method when the program executes. See also dynamic method binding.
lexicographical comparison	a comparison based on the integer Unicode values of characters.
library of classes	a folder that provides a convenient grouping for classes.
line comments	comments that start with two forward slashes (//) and continue to the end of the current line. Line comments can appear on a line by themselves or at the end of a line following executable code. Contrast with block comments.
literal constant	a value that is taken literally at each use. See also unnamed constant.
literal string	a series of characters that appear exactly as entered. Any literal string in Java appears between double quotation marks.
local classes	nested classes that are local to a block of code.
local variable	a variable known only within the boundaries of a method.

Local variable	A variable accessed by the module that declared the variable. A single variable can be both local and global (see Chapter 4).
logic	describes the order of program statements that produce correct results.
logic error	a programming bug that allows a source program to be translated to an executable program successfully, but that produces incorrect results.
Logic structure	A structure for organizing the instructions to the computer that make up a program. There are four logic structures: the sequential structure, the decision structure, the loop structure, and the case structure.
logical AND operator	an operator used between Boolean expressions to determine whether both are true. The AND operator is written as two ampersands (&&).
Logical data	The data set consisting of True and False, used in making yes-and-no decisions.
Logical operator	An operator within an expression that uses logical data as operands and produces logical data as the resultant. The logical operators include NOT, AND, and OR.
logical OR operator	an operator used between Boolean expressions to determine whether either expression is true. The OR operator is written as two pipes (||).
long	the data type that holds very large integers, from − 9,223,372,036,854,775,808 to 9,223,372,036,854,775,807.
loop	a structure that allows repeated execution of a block of statements.
loop body	the block of statements that executes when the Boolean expression that controls the loop is true.
loop control variable	a variable whose value determines whether loop execution continues.
loop fusion	the technique of combining two loops into one.

Loop logic structure	One of the four logic structures for organizing the instructions to the computer that make up a program. The loop structure enables the computer to process the same set of instructions repeatedly.
lossless conversion	a data type conversion in which no data is lost.
lossy conversion	a data type conversion in which some data is lost.
low-level programming language	a language that corresponds closely to a computer processor's circuitry. Contrast with high-level programming language. Compare with machine language.
machine code	machine language.
Machine language	Instructions represented by zeros and ones.
Master file	The file in which all of the data needed for processing are kept current.
Mathematical operator	An operator that uses numeric data as its operands and produces numeric data as the resultant. The mathematical operators include - (subtraction), + (addition), * (multiplication), / (division), \ (integer division), MOD (modulo division), and ^ (power).
matrix	a two-dimensional array.
member-level Javadoc comments	Javadoc comments that describe the fields, methods, and constructors of a class.
menus	lists of user options.
method	a program module that contains a series of statements that carry out a task.
method body	the set of statements between curly braces that follow the method header and carry out the method's actions.
method header	the declaration or first line of a method that contains information about how other methods interact with it.
method's type	the method's return type.
mission critical	a term that describes any crucial process in an organization.

modulus operator	the percent sign; when it is used with two integers, the result is an integer with the value of the remainder after division takes place. Also called the remainder operator; sometimes called just mod.
Multidimensional array	A multidimensional block of elements with a single variable name. Each element is designated by element numbers representing row, column, page, and so on.
multiple inheritance	the capability to inherit from more than one class; Java does not support multiple inheritance.
multiply and assign operator	an operator that alters the value of the operand on the left by multiplying the operand on the right by it; it is composed of an asterisk and an equal sign.
mutator methods	methods that set field values.
named constant	a named memory location whose value cannot change during program execution.
NaN	a three-letter abbreviation for Not a Number.
nanosecond	one-billionth of a second.
nested	describes the relationship of statements, blocks, or classes when one contains the other.
nested classes	classes contained in other classes.
nested if statements	describes if statements when one is contained within the other.
Nested If/Then/Else	A type of decision structure that nests one If/Then/Else instruction within another.
new operator	an operator that allocates the memory needed to hold an object.
nonabstract method	a method that is inherited.
nonstatic member classes	nested classes that require an instance. See also inner classes.
nonstatic methods	methods used with object instantiations. See also instance methods.
nonvolatile storage	storage that does not require power to retain information. Contrast with volatile storage.
NOT operator (!)	the operator that negates the result of any Boolean expression.

null String	an empty String created by typing a set of quotes with nothing between them.
numeric constant	a number whose value is taken literally at each use.
Numeric data	The data type that includes all numbers, integers and real numbers, and is the only data type that can be used in calculations.
object	an instance of a class.
Object class	a class defined in the java.lang package that is imported automatically into every Java program; every Java class descends from the Object class.
Object-oriented programming (OOP)	A language that supports object-oriented principles; a strategy of program design in which the data parts are the principal items, instead of the process.
one-dimensional array	an array that contains one column of values and whose elements are accessed using a single subscript. See also single-dimensional array.
open a file	the action that creates an object and associates a stream of bytes with it.
operand	a value used in an arithmetic statement.
Operator	A sign or symbol in an expression or equation telling the computer how to process the data. The three types of operators are mathematical, relational, and logical.
operator precedence	the rules for the order in which parts of a mathematical expression are evaluated.
optional classes	classes that reside in packages that must be explicitly imported into programs. Contrast with fundamental classes.
out of bounds	describes a subscript that is not within the allowed range for an array.
outer block	a block that contains a nested block.
outer loop	a loop that contains another loop.
overloading	describes using one term to indicate diverse meanings, or writing multiple methods with the same name but with different arguments.
override	to use the child class's version of a field or method instead of the parent's.

override annotation	a directive that notifies the compiler of the programmer's intention to override a parent class method in a child class.
package	a named collection or library of classes. See also library of classes.
Parallel arrays	Two or more arrays in which the data in the same element numbers are related to each other.
Parameter	A variable passed from one module to another module through the calling sequence of the module or function. There are two types of parameters, call-by-value parameters and call-by-reference. Call-by-value parameters cannot be changed in the module. Call-by-reference parameters can be changed and the changed value will be passed back to the calling module.
parent class	a base class.
Parsing	the process of breaking something into its component parts.
passed by reference	describes what happens when a reference (address) is passed to a method. Contrast with passed by value.
passed by value	describes what happens when a variable is passed to a method and a copy is made in the receiving method. Contrast with passed by reference.
passing arguments	the act of sending arguments to a method.
path	the complete list of the disk drive plus the hierarchy of directories in which a file resides.
path delimiter	the character used to separate path components.
pattern String	an argument composed of symbols that determine what a formatted number looks like.
permanent storage devices	hardware storage devices that retain data even when power is lost.
Pointer technique	A programming technique that uses the value in one array to point to an element in another array.

Polymorphism	The ability of an object of various types to respond to method call of the same name and act appropriately.
populating an array	the act of providing values for all of the elements in an array.
Positive logic	A type of decision logic in which the action the computer is to perform follows from the True side of the instruction.
postfix ++ or the postfix increment operator	an operator that is composed by placing two plus signs to the right of a variable; it evaluates the variable, then adds 1 to it. Contrast with prefix ++.
posttest loop	a loop in which the loop control variable is tested after the loop body executes. Contrast with pretest loop.
preferred size	a Component's default size.
prefix ++ or the prefix increment operator	an operator that is composed by placing two plus signs to the left of a variable; it adds 1 to the variable, then evaluates it. Contrast with postfix ++.
prefix and postfix decrement operators	operators that subtract 1 from a variable before and after evaluating it, respectively.
pretest loop	a loop in which the loop control variable is tested before the loop body executes. Contrast with posttest loop.
Primary key	A unique key that is the major key for ordering a file or searching for a record.
priming read or priming input	the first input statement prior to a loop that will execute subsequent input statements for the same variable.
primitive type	a simple data type. Java's primitive types are byte, short, int, long, float, double, char, and boolean.
Print module	A process module that prints the results of processing.
private access	describes a field or method that no other classes can access.
procedural programming	a style of programming in which sets of operations are executed one after another in sequence. Contrast with object-oriented programming.

procedures	sets of operations performed by a computer program.
Process modules	The modules that process the data. They include Calculation, Print, Read, and Data Validation modules.
Program	A computer solution to a problem; a set of instructions in a given computer language that solves the problem.
program comments	nonexecuting statements added to a Java file for the purpose of documentation.
program files	files that store software instructions.
program statements	similar to English sentences; they carry out the tasks that programs perform.
programmer-defined data type	a type that is created by a programmer and not built into the language; a class.
promotion	an implicit conversion.
prompt	a message that requests and describes user input.
property	an instance variable, field, or attribute of a class.
protected access	describes an intermediate level of security between public and private; a class's protected members can be used by a class and its descendants, but not by outside classes.
pseudocode	a tool that helps programmers plan a program's logic by writing plain English statements.
pseudorandom	describes numbers that appear to be random, but are the same set of numbers whenever the seed is the same.
public access	describes a field or method that outside classes can access.
pure polymorphism	the situation in which a single method implementation can be used with a variety of related objects because they are objects of subclasses of the parameter type. See also inclusion polymorphism.
Pushing and popping the stack	Adding (pushing) and taking from (popping) a stack.

Queue	A list in which the next value used was the first one to be added. Data are added and used in a first-in, first-out basis.
ragged array	a two-dimensional array that has rows of different lengths.
random access memory (RAM)	temporary, volatile storage.
random number	a number whose value cannot be predicted.
range check	a series of statements that determine within which of a set of ranges a value falls.
range match	the process of comparing a value to the endpoints of numerical ranges to find a category in which the value belongs.
Read module	A Process module that enters data into the computer.
Record	The set of data for one entity in a file or table.
Recursion	Recursion occurs when a module or a function calls itself.
redeclare a variable	to attempt to declare a variable twice. an illegal action.
reference	a variable that holds a memory address.
reference types	data types that hold memory addresses where values are stored.
Register	A high-speed temporary holding area built into the computer to hold instructions and data needed for the current processing.
Relational operator	An operator within an expression or equation that uses numeric or string data as operands and produces logical data as the resultant. The relational operators include: = (equal to), < (less than), > (greater than), <= (less than or equal to), >= (greater than or equal to), and < > (not equal to).
relative path	a path that depends on other path information to be complete.
remainder and assign operator	an operator that alters the value of the operand on the left by assigning the remainder when the left operand is divided by the right operand; it is composed of a percent sign and an equal sign (%=).

remainder operator	the percent sign; when it is used with two integers, the result is an integer with the value of the remainder after division takes place. Also called the modulus operator.
Report	A formatted output from a program.
Results	The required answers to or output from a problem.
return a value	to send a data value from a called method back to the calling method.
return statement	a statement that ends a method, and frequently sends a value from a called method back to the calling method.
return type	the type of data that, upon completion of a method, is sent back to its calling method.
robustness	describes the degree to which a system is resilient to stress, maintaining correct functioning.
root directory	the main directory of a storage device, outside any folders.
runtime error	an error that occurs when a program compiles successfully but does not execute.
runtime exceptions	unplanned exceptions that occur during a program's execution. The term is also used more specifically to describe members of the RuntimeException class.
scalar	describes simple, primitive variables, such as int, double, or char.
scientific notation	a display format that more conveniently expresses large or small numeric values; a multidigit number is converted to a single-digit number and multiplied by 10 to a power.
scope	the part of a program in which a variable exists and can be accessed using its unqualified name.
scope level	in Java, a variable's block. See also scope.
SDK	a software development kit, or a set of tools useful to programmers; the Java EE Development Kit.
searching an array	the process of comparing a value to a list of values in an array, looking for a match.

Secondary key	A key, which may or may not be unique, that is used to order a file or to search for one or more records in a file. A secondary key is considered a minor key.
seed	a starting value.
seekable	describes a file channel in which operations can start at any specified position.
semantic errors	the type of errors that occur when a correct word is used in the wrong context in program code.
sentinel	a value that stops a loop.
sequence structure	a logical structure in which one step follows another unconditionally.
sequential access file	a data file that contains records that are accessed one after the other in the order in which they were stored.
Sequential logic structure	One of the four logic structures for organizing the instructions to the computer that make up a solution. The sequential structure processes the instructions one after another in a sequence.
Sequential search	A method for locating a record in a file in which the computer starts at the first record and continues through the file, record by record, until the needed record is found.
shadowing	the action that occurs when a local variable hides a variable with the same name that is further away in scope.
short	the data type that holds small integers, from − 32,768 to 32,767.
short-circuit evaluation	describes the feature of the AND and OR operators in which evaluation is performed only as far as necessary to make a final decision.
side effect	any action in a method other than returning a value.
signature	a method's name and the number, types, and order of arguments.
significant digits	refers to the mathematical accuracy of a value.
single-alternative selection	a decision structure that performs an action, or not, based on one alternative.

single-dimensional array	an array that contains one column of values and whose elements are accessed using a single subscript. See also one-dimensional array.
single-precision floating-point number	a type of value that is stored in a float.
software	the general term for computer programs.
Solution	The set of instructions to the computer that will output the results; a computer program before it is coded into a computer language.
Sorting	Arranging data in order; the order may be numeric or alphabetical.
source code	programming statements written in a high-level programming language.
Stack	A list in which the value to be added and the value to be used are on the same end of the list. Data are added and used in a last-in, first-out basis.
stack trace history list, or more simply stack trace	a list that displays all the methods that were called during program execution.
standard arithmetic operators	operators that are used to perform common calculations.
standard input device	normally the keyboard.
standard output device	normally the monitor.
state	the values of the attributes of an object.
static	a keyword that means a method is accessible and usable even though no objects of the class exist.
Static array	An array in which the maximum number of elements cannot change during processing.
static import feature	a feature in Java that allows you to use static constants without their class name.
static member class	a type of nested class that has access to all static methods of its top-level class.

Static method	A method that does not require an object to exist.
static method binding	the opposite of dynamic method binding; it occurs when a subclass method is selected while the program compiles rather than while it is running. See also fixed method binding.
Straight-through logic	A type of decision logic that processes all decisions sequentially, one after another.
stream	a pipeline or channel through which bytes flow into and out of an application.
String class	a class used to work with fixed-string data that is, unchanging data composed of multiple characters.
String variable	a named object of the String class.
strongly typed language	a language in which all variables must be declared before they can be used.
Structure chart	A chart, also called an interactivity chart, showing all of the subtasks, or modules, in a program.
stub	a method that contains no statements; programmers create stubs as temporary placeholders during the program development process.
subclass	a derived class.
subscript	an integer contained within square brackets that indicates one of an array's variables, or elements.
subtract and assign operator	an operator that alters the value of the operand on the left by subtracting the operand on the right from it; it is composed of a minus sign and an equal sign (−=).
subtype polymorphism	the ability of one method name to work appropriately for different subclasses of a parent class.
super	a Java keyword that always refers to a class's immediate superclass.
superclass	a base class.
switch statement	a statement that uses up to four keywords to test a single variable against a series of exact integer or character values. The keywords are switch, case, break, and default.

symbolic constant	a named constant.
syntactic salt	describes a language feature designed to make it harder to write bad code.
syntactic sugar	describes aspects of a computer language that make it "sweeter," or easier, for programmers to use.
Syntax	The rules of setting up instructions and commands in an operating system, a programming language, or an application program.
syntax error	a programming error that occurs when a program contains typing errors or incorrect language use; a program containing syntax errors cannot be translated into an executable program.
system software	the set of programs that manage the computer. Contrast with application software.
table	a two-dimensional array; a matrix. ternary operator an operator that needs three operands.
Term	Definition
text files	files that contain data that can be read in a text editor because the data has been encoded using a scheme such as ASCII or Unicode.
this reference	a reference to an object that is passed to any object's nonstatic class method.
threads of execution	units of processing that are scheduled by an operating system and that can be used to create multiple paths of control during program execution.
throw statement	a statement that sends an Exception out of a block or a method so it can be handled elsewhere.
throws clause	an exception specification in a method header.
TOCTTOU bug	an acronym that describes an error that occurs when changes take place from Time Of Check To Time Of Use.
token	a unit of data; the Scanner class separates input into tokens.
top-level class	the containing class in nested classes.
Traversal	Methods of accessing data within a tree structure.

try block	a block of code that a programmer acknowledges might generate an exception.
two-dimensional array	an array that contains two or more columns of values and whose elements are accessed using multiple subscripts. Contrast with one-dimensional array.
type casting	an action that forces a value of one data type to be used as a value of another type.
type conversion	the process of converting one data type to another.
type-ahead buffer	the keyboard buffer.
type-safe	describes a data type for which only appropriate behaviors are allowed.
type-wrapper classes	a method that can process primitive type values.
unary cast operator	a more complete name for the cast operator that performs explicit conversions.
unary operator	an operator that uses only one operand.
unchecked exceptions	exceptions that cannot reasonably be expected to be recovered from while a program is executing. Contrast with checked exceptions.
Unicode	an international system of character representation.
Unified Modeling Language (UML)	a graphical language used by programmers and analysts to describe classes and object-oriented processes.
unifying type	a single data type to which all operands in an expression are converted.
uninitialized variable	a variable that has been declared but that has not been assigned a value.
unnamed constant	a constant value that has no identifier associated with it. See also literal constant.
unreachable statements	statements that cannot be executed because the logical path can never encounter them; in some languages, including Java, an unreachable statement causes a compiler error. See also dead code.
upcast	to change an object to an object of a class higher in its inheritance hierarchy.

validating data	the process of ensuring that a value falls within a specified range.
variable	a named memory location whose contents can be altered during program execution.
variable declaration	a statement that reserves a named memory location.
virtual classes	the name given to abstract classes in some other programming languages, such as C++.
virtual key codes	codes that represent keyboard keys that have been pressed.
virtual keyboard	a computer keyboard that appears on the screen. A user operates it by using a mouse to point to and click keys; if the computer has a touch screen, the user touches keys with a finger or stylus.
virtual method calls	method calls in which the method used is determined when the program runs, because the type of the object used might not be known until the method executes.
void	a keyword that, when used in a method header, indicates that the method does not return any value when it is called.
volatile storage	memory that requires power to retain information. Contrast with nonvolatile storage.
while loop	a construct that executes a body of statements continually as long as the Boolean expression that controls entry into the loop continues to be true.
whitespace	any combination of nonprinting characters; for example, spaces, tabs, and carriage returns (blank lines).
wildcard symbol	a symbol used to indicate that it can be replaced by any set of characters. In a Java import statement, the wildcard symbol is an asterisk.
wrapped	to be encompassed in another type.
wrapper	a class or object that is "wrapped around" a simpler element.

Index